SECRETS IN
THE ETHER

SECRETS IN THE ETHER

MEMOIRS OF A COLD WAR SPY

ROBERT MINNICK JR.

with Lindy Minnick

SMALL BATCH BOOKS

AMHERST, MASSACHUSETTS

Library of Congress Control Number: 2021923009
ISBN: 978-1-951568-19-1

SMALL
BATCH
BOOKS

493 SOUTH PLEASANT STREET
AMHERST, MASSACHUSETTS 01002
413.230.3943
SMALLBATCHBOOKS.COM

DISCLAIMER

This is a true story. To the best of our knowledge, all the facts are correct. The purpose has been to tell a story of adventure and intrigue that changed the lives of two "brothers"—one from Pennsylvania and the other from Florida—who enlisted in the U.S. Navy in the early days of the Cold War between the U.S. and the USSR. If there are any errors or mistakes in interpretation, the fault is ours.

ROBERT WOOD MINNICK JR., CT3, U.S. NAVY

LINDY MINNICK, FAMILY HISTORIAN

This book is dedicated to
the "Library Ladies"
of the Blountstown Public Library,
Calhoun County, Florida.

CONTENTS

FOREWORD

I n January 2016, I received a response to a holiday card I had
sent my cousin BJ (Robert Minnick, who got the nickname
BJ—short for Bob Jr.). It was in the form of a neatly typed two-
page letter. In this age of social media, texting, and emailing,
it was rare for me to get a personal letter by snail mail. But, as
I would soon learn, BJ was old-school when it came to communicating. He preferred letters and phone calls, as we began
collaborating on our "project." Or maybe it was his training as
an intelligence operative, his realizing how easy it is to intercept and hijack electronic communication. I later learned that
all of the hundreds of original and edited chapter pieces I
received from him were lovingly created by the "Library
Ladies" at the Blountstown Public Library in Florida. And
those same "Library Ladies" had dutifully deleted all his book
material from their computers after his death in 2018. Perhaps
they were just following his instructions. We'll never know.

This is how that letter began:

Lindy, I don't believe I ever mentioned to you or your mom or
Uncle John that I was an intelligence operative in the Navy, working with the NSA and Naval Security Group. I was on Guam for
eighteen months, involved with *Sputnik* and the USSR's missile

submarines operating off Guam and in the Mariana Trench. After my tour, I was assigned to North Africa (Morocco) during the French-Algerian war, where I was involved with General de Gaulle in Algeria as well as monitoring Soviet submarines operating in the Black Sea.

Those four years were extraordinary times for me, and I've never forgotten them, or my two associates. I never knew one of my associates—only that he was an officer who spoke Arabic and French fluently. He was simply our "evaluator" in the field, the field being the Atlas Mountains and Sahara Desert. My other associate, with whom I was stationed on Guam as well, passed away in 2010. I've never really gotten over his passing. He was truly my "brother."

I've been compiling and organizing my thoughts and experiences to create a Minnick family accounting, much like you have done with and for your father. Could you give me some advice and help? It will be so very, very much appreciated.

In 2009 BJ's Naval Intelligence missions were declassified, and he was free to write about them. I promised I'd do all I could to help him create a manuscript; and thus we began our collaboration on his Cold War memoir.

We were on the last chapter of the manuscript when BJ passed away on June 22, 2018. I had received only sketchy snippets from him during his final months. BJ died without telling me how to put the pieces together that would form the last chapter on the Cuban Missile Crisis (CMC) and reveal information, not made public, about the real reason the world did not come to an end in October 1962.

So I have constructed the last chapter as best I could from the snippets he sent me. Everything BJ discusses in this book, all that took place during his four-year career in Naval Intelligence, was a necessary precursor to preventing Armageddon during the CMC. The navy's part in keeping Americans safe from a Soviet nuclear attack in 1962 and beyond never made headlines, but BJ and his Navy "brother," Don Lewandowski (Ski), were convinced of its relevance to the CMC. In one of his last emails to me, BJ remarked, "All of these things—observed, studied, and analyzed—during the course of our four-year tour of duty as Naval Intelligence operatives, enabled us to look at the Cuban Missile Crisis through very different eyes."

Having done my own research into the various records of the events, read Robert Kennedy's account in *Thirteen Days,* and watched countless documentaries on this scary time, I believe there is enough contradictory information to allow for BJ's theory that there was indeed another secret reason for the Soviets to "blink" at the last minute during that stand-off at sea—and turn around at the blockade just off the island of Cuba.

The Cuban Missile Crisis was an event that was complex, fast-moving, and full of deception and deceit from all countries involved. Regardless of the account you choose to believe, the world has never been closer to annihilation before or since. I choose to believe BJ's story that during one of those secret meetings between the U.S. and Soviet leaders, it was matter-of-factly pointed out that the U.S. Navy knew where every single Soviet submarine was hiding and that they were able to detect, track, and disable the threat from every one of them.

A promise is a promise. So, rest in peace, dear cousin BJ. Your Cold War stories will become the memoir you requested—even if that last chapter is not written exactly the way you had envisioned it.

LINDY MINNICK,
San Marcos,
California

SECRETS IN
THE ETHER

ONE

THE SWEET SHOP

It was cold that evening in Tallahassee. It was only October, but it felt like winter was here. Ski and I were trying to find the Sweet Shop, the off-campus favorite eating and meeting place of students, athletes, and cheerleaders at Florida State University. People didn't necessarily come for the food, but the atmosphere was unique. It had been at the same location, 701 West Jefferson, across from FSU, since 1921. It was also *the* place where the varsity football players would gather during a week when no home or away games were scheduled. And this was one of those weeks.

Ski and I had reunited at FSU in 1962, after completing a four-year enlistment in the Navy (1955–1959), the last span being an eighteen-month tour of duty in Morocco, North Africa, at a Naval Intelligence base in Sidi Yahia el Gharb. We had first met at a secret "spy school" located on the "Silver Strand" of Imperial Beach, San Diego, California. We were both sent there from boot camps located almost 750 miles apart (mine in the Great Lakes, Illinois, area; his in Bethesda, Maryland). We had gone through twenty-six weeks of intense communications intelligence training and were given our first eighteen-month tour of duty assignment on Guam, in the

South Pacific, in 1956. We were a team and would become "brothers," working together during our entire four-year enlistment.

Ski and I had played on our Naval base varsity football team on Guam and in North Africa, but we lost both regional championship games to teams from Okinawa in the western Pacific and Châteauroux-Déols Air Base in France. We knew what it was like to play against extraordinary athletes, such as 1954 Maxwell Award–winner and All-American Ron Beagle, a graduate of the Naval Academy in Annapolis, Maryland. Beagle played for the Marine Corps on Okinawa.

Ski was a big guy. He was about six feet four, 240 pounds, while I was the short guy, five feet eight, about 160 pounds. He played offensive/defensive end while I played offensive/defensive halfback in a split-T scheme, which was the prevalent style of play during those times. And we played both offense and defense alternately during the entire game, with the exception of a break or two.

As I said before, it was cold that evening, so we were wearing our Sidi Yahia, Morocco, varsity football award jackets: MacGregor navy blue with a large, three-dimensional golden *N* emblem over the left breast, representing the Navy, and a football emblem on the left arm below the shoulder with the date: 1958. They were classy award jackets, and we were proud of them.

We arrived at West Jefferson Street at the Sweet Shop, and as we rounded a corner, a familiar tune caught our attention. It was the Platters' version of "Smoke Gets in Your Eyes," a recording that we had heard many times back at the base on Guam. I mean, what the hell, I thought everybody knew that all shore-based Naval radio stations had their own amateur disc jockey! And we had spent a good bit of time in the Navy listening to music. Following the sound, we found the front door to the Sweet Shop and walked in. A classic Rock-Ola jukebox from the 1940s was playing the song we'd heard outside. We spotted some open tables in the back of the dining room, past the serving line. There were several large, four-person faux-leather booths between the dining area and the serving line. We noticed that they were all taken by guys who looked like FSU athletes.

As we walked past the first few booths toward the back of the room, a large guy, obviously a football player, called out in a loud voice: "Hey, you guys, come here." Ski and I looked at each other, and he said again, "I said, come over here." We stopped, turned toward the booth where he was seated with three other guys, all of them looking at us. As we approached their booth, the loudmouth said in an even louder voice, "What's with the 'high school Harry' award jackets? You don't wear them at FSU. Didn't anyone tell you that?" Ski and I looked at each other for a few brief seconds while memories of many, many fights over those four years in the Navy—in the barracks, on the liberty bus, in bars, too many places to remember, from Guam to Washington, D.C., to Casablanca, Tangier, Port Lyautey, Gibraltar, and Madrid, Spain—all came flooding back in that short instant. Way too many to remember, and maybe one more here at FSU in the Sweet Shop already. Why not? Been there, done that.

With that, Ski and I moved up to their booth. Then Ski leaned down slightly over the loudmouth, took his index finger, began punching the guy on the bridge of his nose between his eyes, and said, in his deepest northern Pennsylvania accent, "Listen to me, buddy. We were playing football when you guys were sucking your mama's tit." They were stunned.

Then, almost as an afterthought, Ski slowly reached down and turned over the loudmouth's water glass. We watched the water trickle off the table down onto his lap. It was something Ski had done on numerous occasions in the Navy to start a fight, and it usually worked. Except not this time. Not a word was said by anyone. Dead silence. As we turned and started toward our table, all we saw were stares or averted faces.

Then one guy, sitting with his date, said, "Nice job, guys." And as Ski and I sat down, I distinctly heard him say in a muffled voice, "Those guys are two badasses!"

Yeah, that guy was right. I guess we *were* badasses. We were ex–Naval Intelligence operatives, members of the Navy's elite Naval Security Group, the military arm of the National Security Agency in Washington, D.C. We had top-secret clearances; we had conducted top-secret ASW (anti-submarine warfare) monitoring missions in the South Pacific and the Black Sea, as well as guerrilla warfare missions in Algeria during the French-Algerian war.

From that night forward, we wore our letter jackets anytime and anyplace we wanted. Talking about it later that night, we decided that the reason we could not rile those four guys was the simple fact that their coach would probably have dismissed them from the football team for violation of team rules had they responded to our confrontation. And we laughed about it.

So, with this auspicious start, here's our story—from the beginning.

TWO

HAMBURG COVE TO FORT LAUDERDALE

ere my earliest memories are happy ones. I'm a young boy of eight or so, sitting on the dock with my dog Royal Dutch (Roy), fishing while, unbeknownst to me, spirits of ancestors are making silent impressions on my future hopes and dreams.

Meanwhile, behind me is our home, built in the mid-1700s, with low ceilings throughout, a separate outside kitchen connected to the house by a brick walkway, and fireplaces in almost every room. It stands majestically overlooking the Connecticut River. They have done some much-needed renovations on our old home to make it more comfortable—such as walling in the outside kitchen so that using the walkway in full snow gear is not necessary to cook and eat our meals in the winter!

My mother, Nedra, and my father, Robert, are sipping drinks on the front porch, listening to the Billboard countdown of popular tunes of the day, featuring artists such as Perry Como, Frank Sinatra, Dinah Shore, and Bing Crosby. The Andrews Sisters and Benny Goodman play tunes and songs to lift the spirits of war-weary Americans. Many of these artists are fresh off their overseas USO tours, where they have traveled to cheer up and support our exhausted servicemen. I can hear "Sentimental Journey," "Don't Fence Me In," and "On the Atchison, Topeka and the Santa Fe." Mother begins to tap her foot to that last one.

We live in historic Lyme, Connecticut, where winters can be quite harsh. We have moved a few miles north of Old Lyme to Hamburg Cove, a charming and protected area, bounded by high, wooded hills that look much like a fjord with steep green banks in the spring and summer.

As a young boy in the winter of 1946, I remember one morning when it had been snowing lightly since late the night before. My dog Roy, a black springer spaniel, was whining at the living room window, which looked out over an expansive yard and down to the lake in front of our house. The yard was covered in what looked to be some six inches of new-fallen snow down to the remaining few reeds around the small dock on the lake.

A duck lived there, under the dock, in the reeds. He'd been there for some time, ever since my mother had found him injured by some large critter who had caught him and severed his left leg one autumn day over a year earlier. He had survived the attack, been found and rescued by Roy before being almost killed by his attacker. He was a male mallard, obviously on his way south in late autumn, and had the misfortune to land in our lake one afternoon. Mom cared for and fed him almost every day, and in turn, he'd become very dependent upon her. And upon Roy. No one else could get anywhere near him without fear of being "attacked" either physically or verbally (by one hell of a quack)—unless he was in the chicken coop Mom maintained out near the kitchen. That was the only time either I or my brother, Bruce, could get anywhere near him. And we were permitted to get near him only when Roy would allow us to come close. That, to us, was truly amazing.

Well, Roy was still whining, and I started to become alarmed. Where was Mom? I called for her, but no answer. Just as I started to head to the outdoor kitchen, I saw her out of the corner of my eye. She was in the side yard, dressed in my father's rubber waders and large heavy hunting jacket and hat with the earmuffs. The snow was still falling, and she was attempting to walk through the soft snow, which was at least half a foot deep. Then I saw the duck. He was trying to make his way toward Mom through the snow on his good leg, and flapping his wings, which he couldn't get out of the snow. I quickly opened the front door, and Roy sprinted out into the snow, straight down the yard maybe thirty to forty yards, past Mom to the duck. He swiftly circled the duck, patted the snow down, and then patiently lay down beside the helpless duck, known to us only as "Stumpy," as Mom had affectionately called him. Roy was wagging his tail aggressively, and Stumpy was calm. Mom was soon upon the two of them. She gently reached down, picked up Stumpy, and tucked him inside my dad's hunting jacket. With just her arm and Stumpy's head sticking out of the jacket, now nearly covered with snow, she proceeded to carry him across the yard and up to the chicken coop, outside the outdoor kitchen.

When I got there, Mom calmly asked me to open the coop. She entered to a loud cackling and calling by the roughly ten to twelve chickens inside and compassionately placed the duck in his own separate area, filled his bowl with grains and water, turned, and smiled at me and Roy. She patted him, and we went back inside the house. It was a fine morning. A roaring fire in one of the many fireplaces in the house, my dog by my side, and my mother with a big smile on her face. At least for today, she would not give in to the recent sadness that seemed to be crowding out our mostly happy days at the Cove over the preceding few years.

Not much had changed since Dutch explorer Adriaen Block sailed up the Connecticut River in 1614, or since the dugout canoes of the Indians passed over these waters. Hamburg Cove is part of the Eight Mile River, which flows southward from Colchester eight miles downstream through the Cove and into the Connecticut River. It consists of two coves: the Inner Cove, where Cove Landing is located, and the Outer Cove, one of the most charming and protected anchorages in all of New England.

Large schooners brought goods such as molasses and rum from the Caribbean along with fancy textiles to Lyme. In return, they loaded barrel staves, wooden coffin handles, wooden nails, and tinware. In the 1800s they shipped railroad ties "down east" to create the earliest railways, and they brought back granite. As many as one hundred ships a year came to trade goods at the present site of Cove Landing.

Shad fishing has been an important part of Cove Landing's history. The Connecticut River has always been plentiful with fish. In the 1800s the fish caught in Hamburg Cove were delivered to Essex and Deep River for transport to New York City by steamboat. In the 1920s shad fishing was a large part of the economy in Hamburg. During the 1940s there were two dozen fishing boats that could be found fishing along the popular reaches of the river. By 1980, commercial shad fishing in Hamburg Cove had ceased.

While I don't remember the actual move to the Cove, the 1940 federal census places our family on Library Lane—in the heart of Old Lyme, Connecticut. Dad was twenty-eight, Mom was twenty-five, and I was listed as one year old. Our neighbor was Charles Oatley, and his wife, Dorothy, and son, David, seven months. Both Dad and Mr. Oatley listed "fuel oil" as their business, and they were partners in a Shell Oil distributorship near Hamburg Cove that serviced most of Lyme, Connecticut. We would move to Hamburg Cove from our Library Lane house sometime in 1943 or 1944, and it would be an idyllic life for a while.

But was it just a coincidence that we landed in Lyme, Connecticut, when I was in those formative years? I had always known about our Revolutionary War soldier, Abner Smith, who was born in Old Lyme, but not much was known about his family. The two major cemeteries in Old Lyme are Duck River Cemetery and the Old Stone Church Burial Ground. They are filled with our ancestors, and a short walk around town will remind you that many of their descendants still live there today. Visible on street signs, buildings, historical markers, places of business, etc., are such surnames as Marvin, Ely, Huntley, DeWolf, Gee, Smith, Lee, Clarke, Sill, Graham, Champion, and more. The Minnicks can count themselves among their descendants.

The Marvins, the Smiths, the Huntleys, and the Gees of Old Lyme, Connecticut, were very close families. They lived, worked, fought, raised families, worshipped, died, and were buried together. The men in those families were warriors in America's early wars: The French and Indian War, the Revolutionary War, and the Spanish-American War. As hard as everyday life must have been for our ancestors in Old Lyme and Hamburg Cove, they had a strong support system and a belief that anything was possible in this New World. Now it was the 1940s, however, and families weren't as close-knit anymore.

While I was living what I thought was an almost perfect existence for a boy my age, invisible forces in the Cove may have been hard at work fortifying me for a decade of change and a whole lot of pain. As content as I may have been at this time, my parents did not share this feeling of happiness. Even while we were moving into our Hamburg Cove home, world events were spinning out of control.

On December 7, 1941, Japanese warplanes had attacked the home base of the U.S. Pacific Fleet at Pearl Harbor in Hawaii, drawing the United States into World War II. More than 2,300 Americans were killed in that attack. My uncles Bruce and Don Minnick were already in the military. Bruce, single and living in Hartford, Connecticut, working for Connecticut General Life Insurance Company as a clerk, enlisted in the Army on March 17, 1941. Don enlisted in the regular Army Air Corps on August 15, 1941, as soon as he graduated from aviation school in Denver, Colorado. He would marry Adrienne Cavanaugh in 1942 and have a son, Richard Donald, in 1943, before heading off to fight the war over China with a division of General Claire Lee Chennault's Flying Tigers.

My uncle John was studying law at New York University. He rushed down to the Marine Corps recruiting station in the NYC post office the day after Pearl Harbor was hit, and he enlisted in the Marines—without even telling his family. He was called up on January 12, 1942, boarded a troop train in NYC, and landed at Parris Island, where he became a drill sergeant before opting for OCS (Officer Candidates School) at Quantico, Virginia, to gain the skills to lead his men in Pacific Island battles. He married Frances Shears in 1943 and had an infant girl, Lindy, in 1944 while fighting in the Pacific Islands.

The next two years must have put a tremendous strain on the Minnick family and my parents' marriage. In 1945, Grandfather Guy Minnick received two dreaded telegrams from the War Department, notifying him that his youngest son, Donald, was missing in action while flying his P-51 Mustang fighter plane in enemy territory over China while another son, John, had been hit by a mortar shell fragment on Iwo Jima while advancing his men onto the southern edge of Motoyama Airfield Number 2 into the now infamous "Meat Grinder."

My father, Bob, would learn of the death of his youngest brother, Don, as well as the extent of John's battle injuries later that year. The sadness and survivor guilt must have been overwhelming. Bob was the oldest of four Minnick brothers, three of which were serving in active duty in the war. Bob had chosen to serve his country by building submarines in a factory in Connecticut.

In 1946 my father's brother John returned from war, having

lost his left arm just below the elbow. He would undergo months of reconstructive surgery and physical therapy, and he would learn to use a new lifelike artificial hand before he could return to supporting his family and any kind of normalcy. It would be two more years before Uncle Don's body would be located in China and flown back to the U.S. for burial in Arlington National Cemetery.

While recording his own memoirs with his daughter, Lindy, in 2010, Uncle John relived some of that pain felt by the family after Uncle Don's death during the war. He said, "It was no secret that Donny was Mother's favorite"; that "Dad always thought that Donny would become president someday"; and "Brother Bob took it especially hard, and his grief was so great that the family didn't see much of him for a few years."

There would be two more moves for my family. My father moved us to Fort Lauderdale, Florida, in 1947, where he took a job with a Shell distributorship in Miami. Mom and Dad rented a small, two-bedroom, one-bath home across from the Atlantic Ocean just off Atlantic Boulevard (Highway A1A) at 3309 NE 16th Court in Fort Lauderdale. My best memories at that time were the early-morning swims my father and I took every weekday morning before he left for work and after which I would get ready for school. The morning routine would start around 0600, when he would order me into the water, where he'd begin where he'd left off the previous day with my ocean swimming lesson. There was a hell of a lot of difference between an ocean swim and a swim in a swimming pool, believe me, and many times I wasn't looking forward to it. Big waves, undertow, even the venomous Portuguese man o' wars in the surf right up to the beach on the worse days, but relatively calm on a so-called good day. And at my age, around nine or ten, it was always a strenuous task. Learning to swim in the ocean—not a pleasant time.

After my lesson—usually about twenty to thirty minutes, working on stroke and breathing—I'd come out of the water, and he'd start his daily quarter-mile swim up the beach to the Oceania Bar and Restaurant, which adjoined a beachfront motel. I'd run alongside of him while he swam, usually freestyle, followed by the backstroke and finally the breaststroke, or if it was relatively calm, by a strong, powerful freestyle stroke the entire distance. He was extremely athletic and wanted to impart that condition to his son. I like to think he was successful.

When we reached the Oceania, he'd get a cup of coffee; I'd get a glass of orange juice and maybe a doughnut, after which we'd jog back down the beach and home, to get ready for work and the school bus. I truly loved those days,[1] and the lessons were worth their weight in gold, especially when I joined the track team in the tenth grade and later when I joined the Navy in 1955.

When Dad's job in Florida did not work out in 1948, we moved back north, to Saratoga Springs, New York. I regretted leaving Florida and remember that these were difficult and confusing times for me, as my parents separated. Divorce proceedings began in 1949, and I found myself boarding a train in New York City with my mother and younger brother, Bruce. We were bound for Fort Lauderdale, Florida. I would finally get to meet my maternal grandparents, Cecil Leo and Berniece Annis Alexander. Pain and sorrow began to sink in as I learned that we would not be returning to Connecticut but would live with my grandparents in Florida in their two-bedroom, one-bath, ranch-style home that they had built for their retirement years.

We arrived sometime in the midmorning, after the long train ride from New York City to Fort Lauderdale. The weather

---

1. BJ's father abandoned the family shortly after the time of the swimming lessons. BJ was conflicted in his feelings for his father throughout his life. While he admittedly did not relish his early morning plunges into the cold, rough ocean waters, he loved that his dad made time for him and helped him understand the value of being physically fit.

was great: a nice breeze off the ocean, about three miles away, a warm, sunny day, not like the gray, cold day in New York, with snow on the ground. Before we'd gotten on the train in NYC, we'd spent the night with my paternal grandparents, Edna and Guy Minnick, at their big house at 18 Clover Drive, where my dad had grown up in Great Neck, Long Island. I'd been there many times and knew I'd miss seeing them in the days and months ahead.

The train trip had been fun: breakfast and dinner in the dining car and a Pullman sleeping compartment that somehow fit the three of us and provided some degree of privacy to play and move around during the train ride. There was a large picture window that enabled us to see the passing scenery and towns along the way, as we passed the red-light-blinking crossroads and farmlands, which it seems were more plentiful during those times than they are today. But the best part to me was coming into stations and watching the passengers get off and new ones get on.

Grandma and Grandpa Alexander, Mom's parents, met us with a bouquet of gladiolas, and that must have made it a somewhat happier occasion for her. I really didn't know what to expect, but after a short ride, we arrived at their home on Southeast Third Avenue. It was new—built, I believe, in 1946 or so, after his retirement from General Motors in Atlanta, where he had been a regional vice president. The house was built on a triple lot in the city of Fort Lauderdale, utilizing just one of the three lots. The other two were "investments," according to Grandpa. The home was about fifteen minutes from the beach on the Atlantic Ocean. I never knew the story behind our move north from Fort Lauderdale in 1948, but Mother had not been happy in Saratoga Springs.

At the time we had first moved to Florida in 1947, my father had given our two dogs, Royal Dutch and Bunny, away to a close friend in Hamburg Cove, and I never saw them again. They had both been with me since I'd been two years old, and Roy and I were as close as a human and a dog could ever be—playing, squirrel hunting, swimming in the lake in front of our home, romping in the family orchard at Bull Hill, and sleeping in my room at night. To this day, the two dogs have been in my thoughts, never apart from each other.

Anyway, when we arrived at my grandparents' house and walked up to the front door, Grandpa slowly unlocked it, looked inside, and pushed the door open. Standing there at the door, head down to the floor and tail down as well, was "General." He was a brown and white cocker spaniel, somewhat overweight (about twenty-five to thirty pounds), and he appeared to me to be about eight or nine years old. General belonged to my mother's sister Jerry and her husband, Jimmy, who had left him with Grandma and Grandpa while they were assigned to postwar Germany. Jimmy had been a fighter pilot during the war, and although I never knew the story, he may have been attached to the U.S. Air Force leading up to the Berlin Airlift. They'd been gone for roughly a year, and General obviously missed them.

I immediately knelt down to General and took his head in my arms and up to my face. I held him. I missed Royal Dutch. General still was not moving. Mom said he was probably depressed. It seemed to me to be a minute or two at least after I first held his head in my arms and to my chest that he started struggling and moving his head back and forth. And then, to my great surprise, he began to lick my face all over and wag his short tail back and forth very vigorously. Grandpa said that he hadn't seen that behavior in a long time, and it looked to him as though General had found a new friend! I hugged him harder and kissed him in return. He shook himself and looked me directly in the eyes. We just looked at each other for what seemed like minutes.

In that first meeting I became his best friend, keeper, caretaker, and everything else associated with caring for a dog. I fed him every day, took him out for his business in the a.m.

before school and the p.m. after dinner. We went for walks together around the block and over to our ballpark at the local hospital grounds most every day. And once a month, Mom and Aunt Ginny let me take him to the beach with us, where he would frolic in the surf, chase the seagulls and sandpipers, and nip at the baitfish. It was a great love relationship for both of us, one that dramatically helped me handle the depression of not having my dog Royal Dutch or my dad around in those early years following the divorce. I've never forgotten General and our parting nearly a year later.

There had been a lot going on in Fort Lauderdale after the war, as Navy veterans who had previously been stationed at the Naval air station for pilot training returned to sunny south Florida. What made it even harder on all of us was that my mother's sister Virginia (Ginny) had also just been divorced. She decided to move back to Fort Lauderdale from Texas with her two children, Nedra and Chuck, to live with Grandma and Grandpa Alexander as well!

Here we were, the eight of us living in a small, two-bedroom, one-bath home. But the size of the triple lot was to become a lifesaver for all of us. When Grandpa had built his retirement home, he had purchased two adjoining lots, on which we four kids quickly realized we could climb trees, build swings, build forts for imaginary wars, and just play as we wanted. First, Grandpa built a *chikee*—a Seminole Indian structure about fifteen feet by eighteen feet, covered with a thatched palm frond roof, surrounded by orange and grapefruit trees. It was away from the house, so we could always get some privacy.

Grandpa had bought the extra lots for "investment purposes,"[2] but they were really ours for quite a few years; we

---

2. After Grandpa and Grandma passed away in the 1980s, the lots were sold to a group of doctors who were expanding their office near Broward General Hospital.

played sandlot football and baseball there. General especially loved those two lots, with all their slash pines and palmetto bushes, where he'd chase cats and squirrels, hide from us, and suddenly spring out when we crossed his path. During those times, General made a full recovery from his "depression." He lost at least ten pounds and became quite friendly with the neighbor's female dogs; he had to be neutered after some complaints!

I don't recall much about the next part of my "General" story other than to say that one day in either late 1950 or early 1951, Mother took me aside and told me that Aunt Jerry and Uncle Jimmy would be returning from Germany, probably in the next week or two, and they would be taking General back with them to Birmingham. She said she wanted to talk to me about this, and I do recall her taking me and General to the beach later in the week for one last trip before they arrived; that way we could play together on the beach, as we'd done many, many times before. The three of us took off for the beach on a bright but somewhat cool morning. As soon as we arrived, General was at the half-opened window, anxious to get to the water. There was just something about that experience that he loved: running in the sand, into the surf, and back up to our beach blanket, where he'd shake himself off and take off after the seabirds. It was no different this time. As soon as I opened the door for him, he was gone, straight to the water, where he'd bite at and attempt to grab one of the many small baitfish on the shoreline that washed up with each oncoming wave. I just watched, with tears in my eyes, knowing that he'd soon be gone. Then I went down to the shoreline to play with him for the last time. That trip was wonderful, although I remember asking Mom several times if we could "stay just a few minutes more," a request she graciously agreed to. But finally, it was time to leave. It was a silent, wistful drive back to the house, one I didn't want to undertake but had no other choice.

Once back at the house, I gave General his last bath to remove the remnants of sand and salt water all over his body, dried him off with a towel, and let him run. At that moment, I realized that once again in my life, I'd soon be losing my best friend and companion. As I watched him running around the yard, drying himself off, I also realized just how much he had meant to me these many months since we had returned to Florida without my dog Roy and my father, as Mom attempted to cope with her own unhappy life. "Don't take General back," I silently pleaded to my aunt and uncle, who would soon arrive. "Please don't take him from me." I couldn't do much of anything the rest of the day. As I write this, I realize that the time General and I had together somehow enabled me to overcome the great sorrow and pain I'd experienced over my mother and father's divorce. General had been my salvation at this most critical time in my life, and I didn't know how to deal with the looming situation: Now he would soon be gone from my life.

A few days later, Grandpa told us he'd received a Western Union telegram from Uncle Jimmy, advising that they would be arriving soon and would pick up a rental car at Miami International Airport and be in Fort Lauderdale sometime in the early afternoon. They would pick up General and leave for Birmingham shortly thereafter. Upon hearing the news, I can distinctly recall leaving the house, getting on my bike, and riding over to the baseball field at Broward General Hospital, where we played pickup games nearly every day school was out. No one was there, but as I looked around, General suddenly appeared by my side. And once again, I lost it. How do you tell a twelve-year-old boy, "It's okay"? No, it wasn't okay to me. I still hadn't gotten over the loss of Roy, nearly two years earlier, and I knew I'd never get over General either. I threw him my baseball—over and over and over—till he finally returned with the ball one more time and lay down beside me, panting. I waited a few minutes to let him catch his breath and then said, "Let's go, boy, get some water." And we started home.

Aunt Jerry and Uncle Jimmy soon arrived at the house. Most everyone was thrilled to see them, of course—except General and me. He had been with Grandpa and me when they arrived. Grandpa had been comforting me, and I needed it. When the doorbell had first rung, General had stayed by my side with Grandpa, as Mother answered the door. After hugs and kisses, Aunt Jerry saw General and called out to him. He stayed by my side in the far end of the living room, not moving. Again, she called out to him, but he stayed by my side, looking up at me. He didn't move when she called out a third time, and I reached down and patted his head. Uncle Jimmy sensed the situation and called out to General, who remained by my side. Then General stopped, looked up at me—one final look, just the two of us. At that moment, he was my Roy and my General, together once again, the three of us. I teared up, reached down to him, patted his head, and kissed him goodbye. Once again, my heart was broken, and I felt that General felt the same. He slowly walked toward Aunt Jerry and Uncle Jimmy, head and tail down, glanced back at me once more, and he was gone.

As with Roy, I never saw General again, but my heart was broken in 1957, while I was on Guam and learned from my mother of his passing. I believe it was at that moment, as a nineteen-year-old, that I became a man, and later a husband and father. And I've never forgotten those early years with my dog Roy and my dog General. During my troubled youth and throughout my entire life, my dogs—Roy, General, Mijoko, Sydney, Matthaus, Ginger, and Hunter—have given me comfort and love. Many years ago, I heard someone say that "dogs are God's angels." Well, to me, perhaps it could also work another way: Maybe "men are dogs' angels." Who really knows?

Later, Grandpa did some renovations on the house. He

added a dining room extension, a sleeping porch for the three boys, and a TV viewing room. The living situation was getting remarkably better! Still only one bathroom, however.

Although I was surrounded by family in Florida, I missed my dad and our life in Connecticut. I was only eleven years old when he was gone from my life. I felt a lingering loneliness and would not be happy again for quite a few years. The next time I would see my father would be in 1981, thirty-two years later, when he drove from Arizona to Tallahassee, Florida, to see me, my brother, and our children. It wasn't a pleasant trip for him healthwise, and he only stayed for two days before heading back home. He left us with some photographic memories of the past, a small amount of money for the children, and he was on his way.[3]

I was shy and reserved, kept to myself in school, and didn't participate in sports with the exception of VFW youth football and baseball, which I greatly loved. Soon all that would change dramatically.

I was in my ninth-grade mechanical drawing class at Fort Lauderdale High School in the spring of 1953, when I was fourteen, minding my own business. I didn't see him at first, but one of the class bullies walked up to me and, without warning, let me have it. Next thing I knew I was on the floor, my nose bleeding profusely, my right eye closing, and two front teeth loose and about to fall out.

Our teacher, Mr. Kendrick, helped me up, told the guy who hit me to sit down until he got back, and helped me down to the nurse's office. After she cleaned and bandaged me up, she let me ride my bike home—about five or six

---

3. Robert Wood Minnick Sr. passed away on April 23, 1985, in Davenport, Iowa, at age seventy-four. He is buried in Pine Hill Cemetery, Davenport, Iowa, Section 1, Lot T, G58.

blocks. She had attempted to call my mother but got no answer.

My mother almost freaked out when she saw me. And I don't even want to think about what she attempted to say. When Grandpa Alexander returned from work that afternoon, he just looked at me and went about his business. As soon as dinner was over, though, Grandpa took me out to the carport and had me get up into the alcove above the carport floor, open his storage trunk, and take out two pairs of boxing gloves. He then proceeded, over the next month or so, to teach me how to throw a left hook, his favorite punch.

I was fourteen, in the ninth grade, five feet six, and probably weighed around 130 pounds. Grandpa was somewhere in his sixties, about five feet eleven, and considerably heavier than I was. But from the beginning, he made me throw my left-hand punch, and he'd always block it somehow. I didn't know it at the time, but that was the key. I needed to learn how to counter a block while also avoiding a punch from my opponent. Not an easy task, believe me. It took some time before I was able, first, to recognize a punch or counterpunch coming at me and, second, to react quickly with my left.

The left hook was to become my best and, in most cases, my *only* punch. It took me many, many times before I could block Grandpa's right-hand downward while at the same time throwing my left. But when I did get the left hook off ahead of his right lead, I was always successful in connecting squarely with his unprotected right jaw. Moreover, after probably two or three weeks, I could mostly always hit him before his right even got close to me.

Then there was that day a month or so later, when I really, for the first time, connected with my left to his jaw solidly and with strength. He immediately let me know that I had finally learned how to throw the punch, and with a little more practice and aggressiveness, I'd never again be at a disadvantage against anyone, larger or smaller than myself. I'd learned how to defend myself. In fact, over the years in the Navy, I found myself able to throw the left hook ahead of an aggressive right-hand lead or to block an attempt by my opponent. I got the same result when my opponent was a left-hander. Grandpa had said that for me, with my size and style, this manner of throwing the left hook, which he termed a "power left hook," would be my best offensive punch. It truly was. It was the kind of punch an opponent never would have expected, and that had been Grandpa's intent all along. I was forever grateful to him for being there for me in my adolescence, when I needed someone the most.

I later learned from Grandma that Grandpa had participated in Golden Gloves boxing many years before in Detroit. He taught me how to feign, how to distribute my weight properly, how to step up when throwing the punch, and—best of all—how to beat a guy to the punch. He also got me a set of dumbbells, which I had to use every day. Finally, he taught me how to skip rope so I could move quicker. I was starting to feel happier.

All during this time, I'd been watching the bully, observing his every move when he was around me. So, a few months later, this same bully came up to me again in mechanical drawing class. As he raised his right, I stepped forward toward him, and I hit him with a left hook squarely on the right side of his face, on his jaw, and he dropped like a sack of potatoes. The class was silent, and Mr. Kendrick said to me very quietly, "Bob, please take your seat." Man, was I one proud and happy camper! That bully, or anyone else, never bothered me again. That was some punch. . . . Thanks, Gramps! I became a confident fourteen-year-old. Shortly thereafter, when track tryouts began, I tried out, made the squad, and ran the sprints (100-, 200-, 400-, and 800-yard relays) like my father had done in high school and college (Amherst). I was one of the top two sprinters.

Everything seemed to be just fine now. It was the first

weekend in January 1954, and I got my first real job. Never mind that it was a part-time one with no pay. It was just what I had been waiting for: I was a mate on a charter sport fisher at Bahia Mar Yacht Basin on the Intracoastal Waterway across A1A from the beach in Fort Lauderdale, one of roughly twenty to twenty-five other charter boats in the fleet catering to snowbirds from up north.

I'd gotten an Allstate scooter for Christmas and a coveted job as a mate on the forty-five-foot sport fisher *High Hopes*. She was a Florida-made boat, a Huckins twin-diesel, fourteen-foot beam, wood-hulled, upper-controls cockpit tower, and she had between twenty-eight-foot and thirty-foot outriggers. A real beauty. Nice salon, galley, captain's quarters, and head as well as a very spacious fishing pit. But that scooter is what made this Christmas great. Without it, I had no way to get to work as a mate at 0600 on Saturdays and Sundays.

The weekend job required my presence from 0600 to roughly 2030, and it did not provide any pay. But the tips were great and more than made up for lack of a paycheck. We even got to sell whatever fish the charter party didn't take, to the large number of "lookers" who were around after the charter party had left.

To get one of those jobs, you had to be a high school student, have some experience, and have a guaranteed way to get to work each weekend morning at the crack of dawn. Monday-to-Friday mate jobs were all full-time, held by fully qualified mates. I was really lucky that my high school in Fort Lauderdale had little competition—only the small Catholic school, Pinecrest, and the Black high school, Dillard, which had just been newly rebuilt four miles from the Old Dillard School (which is now a Black history museum).

This was an extremely demanding job! Arrive at sunrise, prepare drinks and snacks, rig rods and reels, set up the "pit" (usually the two permanent fishing chairs and two temps), raise the outriggers, ice down the fish box, check the engine room and bilge pump batteries, and prepare the leaders, bait, etc. A tough job, but I loved it!

There wasn't much time between the a.m. and p.m. charter groups. In addition to helping the a.m. party gather their carry-on stuff and get off the boat, I had to dress out the fish we'd caught, ice and pack the fillets for them, do a quick wash-down of the pit area and clean up any vomit I'd missed earlier, spray Pine-Sol in the salon and head area (especially where someone had puked where I hadn't noticed it), and clean up all the "trash" they always left behind. By then the noon charter had arrived, and we started the routine all over again. Fortunately, most of the "real" anglers chartered the all-day trips Monday through Friday.

The time after the p.m. charter was a real killer. That's when we had to give the boat a complete saltwater and fresh-water wash-down from bow to stern, clean inside and outside, and towel it all down to get ready for the next day's charter. First, however, we had to dismantle the rods and reels, clean them, and return them to the rod racks on the salon ceiling. Next, we stored the temporary fishing chairs; wiped down and soaped out the pit; soaped and watered out the fish box, bait box, and entire transom area; and rechecked the engine room, bilge pump, batteries, life preservers, flags, and the head. Lastly, we cleaned the windows and portholes, etc.

By the time 2030 rolled around, we weren't in any mood to party across the street on the beach with our friends, who usually got together on Saturday and sometimes Sunday nights. Besides, we were just too damn tired, period. But it was extraordinarily fun and satisfying. We made good money on the tips and got one hell of a workout all at the same time. Couldn't beat that!

Something else I remember about my job as a mate on this charter boat: When I was being interviewed and asked if I had any experience, I said that since I was eight years old, I had gone deep-sea fishing in the summer with my dad in the

Atlantic for blues, and in the spring with him on the Connecticut River for shad. Living in Hamburg Cove, just up the coast from Saybrook, where Dad and Charles Oatley kept a small boat in a Saybrook marina, would serve me well in more ways than I could imagine at the time of that interview. I had learned a lot about fishing on those trips out of the marina with my dad. At that young age, I learned how to catch those fish, clean them, and remove the roe from the shad. When I mentioned removing the roe, my interviewer immediately asked the one question he dreaded asking every applicant, "Do you get seasick?" to which I replied, "No sir, I don't." I was hired on the spot! Now that I think about it, that's probably one of the reasons I joined the Navy.

Let me tell you something about deep-sea fishing: There are several types of trolling when it comes to catching fish, depending on your environment and the type of fish you are after. Our environment was the Gulf Stream, roughly ten miles off the coast of Fort Lauderdale. It flows from near the Keys south of Miami, up the East Coast hundreds of miles, until it turns right and crosses the Atlantic. The Saturday or Sunday tourist trip begins in the a.m. or the p.m., with a four-hour trip being the most successful, given that we're out to catch the most edible fish in the shortest time for a party that more often than not is on its first or second deep-sea fishing trip while on vacation. This scenario calls for what charter boat captains refer to as "regular" trolling: dead bait (usually ballyhoo or mullet) for kingfish, dolphin, or wahoo (pelagic fish that are considered the best from a charter perspective for eating). In regular trolling, the boat is moving along slowly between six to eight knots, along a "grass" or "weed" line (in our area, sargasso weed from the Sargasso Sea, composed of algae and small crustaceans, sought after by small baitfish) at the edge of the Gulf Stream, where baitfish congregate. The bait we're trolling is usually ballyhoo, about seven to nine inches long, which has been rigged so it appears to a prospective catch to be live bait on the surface of the water—two or more baits in a V pattern about fifty to seventy-five yards behind the boat.

Rigged ballyhoo makes a great presentation to any predator fish in the immediate area. This method of fishing from a charter boat, in contrast with drifting or stationary fishing, offers a much better chance of hooking up with a good fish—first, because we are covering more area and, second, because we are relying on a "reaction" strike, so called because the fish simply strikes the bait violently and ingests it at the same time, unlike the sailfish, which kills or stuns the bait with its bill prior to ingesting the bait. This is also why you use an outrigger to catch sailfish, because the sailfish strikes the bait with its bill, causing the line to release from the outrigger and stop moving in the water for a few seconds, simulating "dead" bait.

So trolling works well when fishing for kingfish, dolphin, or wahoo—although you'll probably need a little more speed, perhaps twelve to sixteen knots, to attract the wahoo, which is considered one of the fastest and most aggressive fish in the ocean. In my experience, a wahoo will nearly always aggressively attack a trolled bait, more so than will a kingfish or a dolphin. But then again, this is merely my experience. More than a few times, a dolphin will just play with the bait, rather than ingesting it immediately, while a king will do most anything.

One more bit of information I want to share with you when you're fishing. It comes from my knowledge about ASW (anti-submarine warfare) during the time I was in the Navy. Sounds of virtually any form transmitted into the water can either repel or attract fish. This is partly due to the fact that sound travels roughly five times faster in water than it does in air and that fish are extremely sensitive to a wide range of frequencies. Science has shown that a fish will rarely ever swim toward an alarming sound. However, the generally quiet

splash of a bait, such as a rigged ballyhoo, at a respectful distance from the fish will often attract its attention rather than
spook it. A fish doesn't have ears like humans and other mammals do, but it does have "ears" called "otoliths," buried in
either side of its head and protected by skin, flesh, and bone.
In addition, a fish has a second sound-detecting organ known
as the "lateral line," which is unique in the animal kingdom.
This system runs along the length of its body. Vibrations in
the water pass through thousands of "openings" along the
lateral line, which alert the fish to the sounds. The lateral line
works within a range of twenty to thirty feet from the fish. As
the fish gets closer to the source of the sound (the baitfish,
etc.), it can locate its prey even if it can't yet see it. If the fish
gets within roughly five feet or so, it can accurately strike the
baitfish without actually seeing it.

Accordingly, sound plays a vital role in the daily activities
of fish. Using their "ears" and their lateral line, they can detect
any disturbance in the water and react to it, whether it is food
or a predator ready to attack them. So, from a fishing point of
view, the key to success lies in reducing or eliminating alarming sounds. People on the boat can talk all they want, as loud
as they want, and the sounds of their voices will bounce off
the surface of the water. But scrape a tackle box or bang your
feet on the deck of the boat, and the noise will transmit
through the water. This is especially true in clean, shallow
water, such as the flats; if you drop a lure too close to a tar-
pon or bonefish, you can bet you're screwed because nine out
of ten times, you'll spook the fish. Even if the fish doesn't go
far, it will be on alert, and it will be difficult to get it to strike
your bait.

In summary, you need to be aware of the effects of sound
on fish and make sounds work for you, both in attracting fish
and avoiding those sounds that frighten them or alert them
that something is not right. One final thought: Bonefishing in
certain areas of Florida and the Bahamas is extremely popular,

and knowledgeable fishing guides are well worth the price they charge, so beware, and good luck.

On a Sunday in early January 1954 (the second day of the season and my second day as a mate), Captain Bill Williams of the forty-five-foot sport fisher *High Hopes* at the Bahia Mar Yacht Basin said the weather that day was about the same as the day before. Sunny, winds out of the northeast at about eight knots, seas running three to four feet offshore and a little more in the Gulf Stream at relatively calm winds. Seemed almost ideal to me, although of the three conditions, wahoo (which is my favorite catch) prefer it a bit rougher. For them, we'd like it to be a higher-speed troll of about twelve to sixteen knots.

Our party that day was a dad, a mom, and their son, twelve years of age. They weren't experienced, although the dad had been out a few years earlier with some friends. This was their first trip to Fort Lauderdale, and they were really looking forward to the fishing trip, in celebration of their son's twelfth birthday. Captain Bill Williams started the engines as I untied the dock lines from their cleats. At the same time, the marina attendant released the bow line and threw it to me, and I undid the stern lines. Bill eased the *High Hopes* out of her slip and into the Intracoastal Waterway toward the Pier Sixty-Six Marina fueling docks, where we'd top off the fuel tanks with diesel fuel and fill the water tanks. Soon we were on our way. I noticed that the wind was out of the east, about ten to twelve knots, the sky was clear, the air temperature about seventy degrees, just a light chop on the Intracoastal Waterway, and two or three other charters on the way to the Gulf Stream. I started preparing the fishing tackle for what I hoped would be a great day on the water. To my way of thinking, every day in the Stream was a great day.

I had everything prepared for the trip, and in no time, we were making our way out of the port channel, past the Coast Guard station and the jetties, and into the open water. About ten minutes later, with the beach still in sight, the port rod, where the boy was sitting, started singing. I jumped back from the fish box, grabbed the rod out of the rod holder, tightened the drag to slow the fish, and set the hook good; within just a minute or so, our catch had stripped forty or fifty yards off the Fin-Nor reel. It was a good-size fish, more than likely a twenty-to-twenty-five-pound king, just about right for a great meal. I gave the rod to the boy and showed him how to lean forward, pull up on the rod, and let it go forward while reeling in the line. He was on his way to a great birthday!

I had his dad reel in his line and sit back to enjoy his son's battle. His mom was ready with the camera. This boy was really excited! About fifteen minutes later and several runs, we had a nice twenty-five-to-thirty-pound king alongside the transom, and I was prepared to gaff it. I hit him right behind the gills and got him inside the boat and into the fish box, where he was giving it hell with his flapping. Meanwhile, I got the dad's line back in the water. I had hardly gotten the line in the water when his line started screaming off the reel. I went through the routine again, assisting him as he tightened the drag, got the rod situated in the rod holder, set the hook, and started fighting the fish. It was about an eighteen-to-twenty-pound king this time. Two happy fishermen, with two nice fish in the boat, and we'd only been fishing for about thirty minutes!

The mom took her pictures. The boy ate the first of numerous snacks that morning, and we settled in for the final twenty-minute ride to the Gulf Stream. About this time, I began thinking about my wahoo chances. That's what I really wanted to catch. Catching a wahoo is an ordeal in itself, and to be truthful, once you've caught one, that's all you'll really want to catch again. There is a world of difference between fighting a twenty-five-to-thirty-pound king or dolphin and a similar-size wahoo. I think we caught three or four more fish—king and dolphin but no wahoo. Everyone was pleased, especially Bill, who gave me quite a bit of praise once we got in.

Music has always been a significant part of my life. I think it's because Grandmother Alexander was a concert pianist in her younger days in Detroit, and with my mother being the oldest of her four children, she hoped that perhaps my mom would take up the piano at some time in her young life. She did, but not to the extent that Grandmother would have liked. Mom was an excellent pianist, in my somewhat biased opinion. When Mom was in her early teens, Grandmother Alexander suffered a serious fall down the stairs to their basement. She severely fractured her left wrist and was never able to regain her competency on the piano; she had to forgo her career. When Mom, Bruce, and I arrived in Fort Lauderdale back in 1949 (after Mom left my father), one of the first things we saw in Grandma and Grandpa's house was Grandma's Steinway grand piano. For whatever reason, she simply could not let go of her piano, and it had a place of honor in the living room of their new retirement home in Fort Lauderdale.

We lived with them for nearly four years, and Mom took up the piano almost from the day we arrived in the spring of 1949. By the summer she had written a song for the small town of Lauderdale-by-the-Sea, a beautiful enclave of homes just off the beach between Fort Lauderdale and Pompano Beach, across A1A from the Atlantic Ocean. I don't recall the story of how or why she became involved in writing the song, but I do remember her working diligently on it from those early days. But here's the best part of the story: Mother had found something good to do that comforted her—after many years, I'm sure. And I found myself sitting on the piano bench with her, watching and listening to her play. She would play popular music, including my favorite, "White Christmas," and she would start playing the Christmas music usually a day or so after Thanksgiving, when Grandpa would go out to buy the Christmas tree. It was an extremely big and tall tree—at last ten feet.

Nearly every night until Christmas Eve, Mother would play a medley of tunes from late afternoon until dinner at 1800. Her playing music nearly every afternoon eventually evolved into somewhat of a "cocktail hour," when Aunt Ginny, together with Ann and Chuck Holden (our next-door neighbors who had two sons about the same age as Ginny's children, Nedra and Chuck), would all gather around the piano. All four of us kids loved those times. From the "cocktail hour" grew a Saturday afternoon ritual (like a "gig" among friends, which included George Wiesman, who later married my mom) at Brownie's Bar, a small neighborhood bar off Southeast Third Avenue in Fort Lauderdale, about a mile from Grandma and Grandpa's house. Mother would play the piano, George the clarinet, and Chuck Holden the sax. Unfortunately, sometimes they'd stay for happy hour and finally get home around 2100 or 2200. All in all, good times for Mother and Aunt Ginny and us kids.

I think that time period, with all Mother's piano work, was the primary reason why I love music so much, although I never played an instrument. Bruce later played the trumpet in the high school band after we moved to Pompano Beach. Chuck played the drums in a five-man band during high school, mostly at the youth center in Fort Lauderdale Beach. He became an excellent drummer and had all the girls chasing after him! Playing after high school in several local bands, Chuck played the music of the day—such as that introduced by Dick Clark and many DJs of the 1950s. Finally, in the late '50s, there was my Navy "brother," Don Lewandowski. Ski played the harmonica, and damn well if I do say so. In fact, it's one of the reasons why in "BJ's Song" I have a harmonica as one of the instruments.

Things were going well. I was finally happier. Before the fight in ninth grade, I had been a quiet, reserved, and somewhat shy type of guy. But now I was an athlete, I was a better student, and for the first time I had a girlfriend. Her name was Martiel Congleton, and she was my first real love. All my work in the Navy would be identified by her initials, "MC." Time was passing quickly.

Mother married George Wiesman, a Fort Lauderdale architect, in 1952, and by 1955 we had moved to Pompano Beach, Florida. George was opening a new architectural design office there in anticipation of rapid growth in that area. Mother seemed content to settle into her new life with George in Pompano Beach, and my brother, Bruce, was just starting junior high school. I was missing all my friends on the track team back at Fort Lauderdale High, as well as grieving the loss of my girlfriend, Martiel. Maybe I just wasn't thinking clearly (or maybe I just gave myself over to the "spirits of the Cove" for guidance), but right then and there, I decided to join the Navy rather than attend a new high school for my senior year.

The next thing I knew, I was being sworn into the Navy in Jacksonville, Florida, and I was boarding a train to Chicago. Waking up the next morning, I was at the gates to the U.S. Naval Training Center (Naval Station Great Lakes) in Waukegan, Illinois, and I was thinking, *What the hell have I done?*

THREE

NAVY BOOT CAMP

Six of us from the Fort Lauderdale, Florida, area arrived at the U.S. Naval Training Center (Naval Station Great Lakes), Waukegan, Illinois, around 1000 hours, Friday, July 15, 1955, exactly three days after my seventeenth birthday. You had to be seventeen to enlist, and I'd done it. It had been a long, overnight trip from Jacksonville, where we were sworn into the Navy and completed our preliminary physical examination. I wondered what the Navy would have done if I had failed the physical exam. How would I get home and, most worrisome, what would I tell everyone? Jesus, that would have been hell. But I passed, so the pressure was off—for now.

I don't think any of us slept a minute the previous night on the train, and we were feeling pretty raw. We'd been in coach, and we carried on way too much, even though we couldn't get hold of a beer. Not one. I know that quite a few passengers were fed up with us by the time we arrived in Chicago. I think we came in at Grand Central Station on the Chicago Loop, where we got a commuter train to Waukegan. All I remember is that we got a train directly to the Naval Training Center. And when I got there, my first thought upon seeing the size and scope of the place, some seven hundred buildings spread over a thousand-plus acres, was *What the hell have I done now?*

When I'd left Fort Lauderdale, I'd given up Sundays on the beach with my friends, my mate's job on the *High Hopes* during the winter months, money in my pocket, my caddy job at my stepdad's golf course, and the guys on the track team. My buddy had just gotten a 1949 Ford convertible, which he spent every minute with, so he sold his 1950 Harley-Davidson 125cc to me for fifty dollars. I was leaving my newly acquired motorcycle behind, and I also gave my Allstate scooter to my next-door neighbor buddy in Fort Lauderdale.

But the hardest of all was saying goodbye to my girlfriend, Martiel. In fact, I had a picture of her on the *Emerald Seas* cruise ship with three other girls on a cruise to Nassau, Bahamas, on which she had written, "Don't worry, I'll come around someday." To this day, I don't know what she really meant by that. But I've fantasized about it for all these years. And I still have the picture. In fact, I went a step further and used her initials, "MC," as my code letters when I got to Imperial Beach after boot camp at the CT (cryptologic technician) intelligence school, for which I was selected as my Navy billet. I kept those two letters throughout my entire Navy enlistment.

Speaking of intelligence school, how in the world did I end up there? With a top-secret military clearance, working for the National Security Agency in Washington and the Naval Security Group? I'll tell you about that shortly, but right now I want to let you know what a recruit goes through when he or she joins the military as an enlisted person. I had packed my civilian clothes—pants, shirts, and shoes—for shipment home after we got our uniforms, and the transition from civilian to military life was over.

New recruits were administered their first of numerous shots, measured and sized for uniforms, given a butch haircut and preliminary dental exam, and told to undress for the infamous crotch test for hernia and hemorrhoids. Next, we got a recruit training company assignment (mine was Company 389, Recruit Training Command). I put my "stuff" in the area designated "Company 389") and kept moving. Next, we moved to the clothing area, where we picked up our initial uniforms: dress whites, dress blues, dungarees, shoes, socks, military underwear, rainwear, winter peacoat, "cover," pillow, mattress cover (called a "fart sack"), and Navy swimsuit. Quite a list. *Note:* When we picked it up, all we had to do was put it on. The clothing had already been tailored to pants, 34W, 29L; shirts, 15½ x 32; T-shirts, 38; underwear, 32–34; etc.—and our "cover," 6½ or 7, whatever. Not a bad system, extremely quick and precise. Also, shoes, size 8 "E." Now that we had all this gear, we stored it under our company designation "389," along with several stencils of our names—that would come later, in the barracks.

The last item was the seabag, the Navy's idea of a suitcase. From there we picked up three books: the Bible, *The Blue-jacket's Manual,* and *The Recruit Workbook*; we put our name and service number in them and moved on to the last item on that first day's agenda: the recruit classification area. Here we underwent an initial battery of tests and were personally interviewed again (the first time had been back home at the recruit enlistment station in Fort Lauderdale). We then "fell out," to march to our assigned barracks. Our first responsibility as a seaman recruit when we got to our barracks—which we still hadn't seen—was to stencil and put on our uniform correctly—especially our "cover," the Navy's white cap to a civilian—followed by our learning how to recognize and salute a Naval officer, how to use the manual of arms, and other normal military duties and customs. It made for a long day, to say the least. Next up was the chow hall! Not a bad meal.

In the Navy, the time in rank was predetermined before possible promotion: seaman recruit, nine months; seaman apprentice, nine months; seaman, nine to twelve months; noncommissioned officer (i.e., communications technician third-class [CT3], twelve months, etc.). Boot camp itself was eight weeks. In certain billets, such as Naval Intelligence, you could move up faster through the ranks by taking special exams or, better yet, by receiving "proficiency pay" based strictly on performance (which Ski and I received in North Africa) in addition to "hazardous duty" pay or "TDA" (temporary duty assignment on submarines) pay on Guam.

One of the numerous occupational tests we had to take to be assigned a military billet was a foreign language aptitude test. The test was one recently adopted by the Navy called "Esperanto," for testing a recruit's ability to learn a foreign language. It was relatively easy to learn and allowed people who speak different languages to communicate with each other (so we were told). In fact, the instructor said it would take only a fraction of the time it took to learn most other languages. I'd had the equivalent of about six months of Spanish in high school, if that, but believe me, it didn't help me one bit with this test. And I still didn't believe that any of the sixty guys in our company knew why it was necessary for us to take a language aptitude test in the Navy.

Roughly a week or so later, five or six of us were told we were going to take the test again in a somewhat different version. My first thought was *What? Why me?* I didn't think I'd done particularly well on the first test, but I had no choice. As it turned out, I must have done better than I thought I had the first time I took the test because I completed it this time without much trouble. Maybe because I was "familiar" with it by then—who knows? Next thing I knew, I was taking a Morse code test, and that wasn't much easier. But I remembered that when I'd worked on the *High Hopes* charter fishing boat back in high school, I'd been intrigued with the Coast Guard's Morse code transmissions I heard constantly on the ship-to-shore radio on board among all the chatter between charter boat captains. Turns out, I also did well on the Morse code test, but I had no idea of what value it would be, except maybe to be a radio operator on a ship or something like that.

There were six or seven other tests I took over the eight-week period in boot camp, and around the time we'd reached the final week, we were told, as a group, what our first duty station was to be. Most of the guys had been assigned to various Naval schools—i.e., aviation mechanic, gunner's mate, quartermaster, etc.—while the others were directly assigned to ships or shore-duty stations for on-the-job training in various capacities.

I was in a different category for some reason. Our company commander didn't even call out my name. What in the hell was this all about? When I asked him, "What about me?" I was informed that I would pick up my orders on the morning we all left boot camp, in three or four days. I was absolutely stunned. What? I'd had a good relationship with our company commander, volunteered and boxed for the company, ran the sprints—did well, I thought, on all the training activities over the past seven weeks. What was going on?

About ten to fifteen minutes later, when he'd finished answering questions from some of the guys about their billets, he called me over and told me that I would be going over to recruit command headquarters, personnel section, and would ask to see enlisted classification record NavPers-601, a form in my records that indicated the Navy's recommendation for further assignment upon completion of boot camp. The next morning, he gave me permission to go over to the personnel section office. In a few minutes, I had a file in hand. I had been recommended to strike for "electronics operator ratings." Then I saw it: I had volunteered for "CT duty," and I had signed with my full signature and initialed the form on August 15, 1955—roughly three weeks earlier. I didn't remember having done that. And what was "CT duty" anyway? Little did I know that my billet was NAVSECGRU 11111. I was going to an intelligence school, where I would be trained as a "CT-R branch intelligence operative" with the Naval Security Group.

Nor did I know that during the next three years of my enlistment, I would be TDA (temporary duty assignment) aboard a submarine in the Mariana Trench off Guam in the South Pacific among "many" Soviet submarines; on the Sahara Desert in North Africa during the French-Algerian war, conducting covert shortwave radio-intercept missions involving an assassination plot on the life of General Charles de Gaulle; continuing ASW (anti-submarine warfare) monitoring duties in the Black Sea;[4] and ultimately, when I was out of the Navy, coming face to face with the Cuban Missile Crisis of October 1962 and the very real threat of "Armageddon."

Back to those days at the U.S. Naval Training Center at Waukegan, Illinois, I was a seventeen-year-old who had decided to skip his senior year of high school, join the Navy, see the world, and become a man! We spent hours in class, learning the basic principles of seamanship, gunnery, discipline, firefighting, and multiple other Naval subjects. There were many tests: GCT, ARI, Mech, Electronics, Languages, Clerical, Qualified Swimmer, Radio, and much Physical Readiness.

We also had organized athletics and company competition. I volunteered to box for the company and run the sprints. I've never forgotten the time when Grandpa taught me how to box; it was then and still is one of the pivotal points in my life. And now, in Navy boot camp in 1955, I was first to volunteer to box for our recruit company after our company commander asked for some sailors to represent the company in athletic competition—in some track and field events, wrestling, boxing, and basketball.

I won my share of the sprints and three of my five boxing matches. One loss was to a guy who was just a much better

4. BJ's duties consisted of monitoring Soviet submarines in the Black Sea from his Navy base in North Africa.

boxer than I was, and the other loss was to a guy who came out of the corner with both arms flailing like a windmill, never stopping. I finally asked the referee, "Make him fight me, ref. He's fighting like a girl." The ref didn't say a word, so I climbed out of the ring after the first round and forfeited. I knocked the other three guys to the mat several times with my left hook, and I won all three by decisions. One other point: We had to wear headgear in the ring and had heavyweight gloves, so it wasn't much of a fight anyhow. That's how it all started for me and Ski, and I went on to get into many barroom and barracks fights over the next four years on Guam and in North Africa. Just part of the way it was in the Navy. Thank God for my grandfather.

Our company had survival swimming, Naval teamwork, and esprit de corps. Training symbolized both the self-reliance of the individual and the teamwork of the group. About 50 to 60 percent of the company would go on to schools and further specialized training. The rest would go directly to ships and shore stations around the world, to begin on-the-job training and duties in fulfilling the Navy's mission.

Each company had sixty recruits, directed and trained by a petty officer first-class or a chief petty officer (both noncommissioned officers), who served as the company commander. Our lives as Navy recruits were very competitive from the beginning, and the company commander would even turn his head away or walk out of the barracks whenever a fight broke out. He was like a father, and he wanted us to become *men*! Now.

We got a real surprise that afternoon. Our company commander told us that after dinner that night we would return to the barracks and get ready for an evening out. We would be going to the base enlisted men's club for a dance hosted by a high school girls' organization that, on Friday nights, held a dance for sailors in their final two weeks of boot camp, complete with disc jockey and dance music, soft drinks and snacks—no beer, unfortunately. It would be in dress white uniforms and polished shoes—and he meant *polished*. It would last from around 2100 to 2300. Most of the guys were excited, although I felt pretty bad. I still hadn't gotten over the loss of Martiel that last week in Florida before I'd left for boot camp. The dance was mandatory, so I had no choice in the matter but to go.

When we got to the enlisted men's club, the girls had already arrived. I was surprised. These were fine-looking girls, most in their last year of high school or beginning students at the local junior college. They appeared to be really friendly. My cubicle mate and I picked out two we thought were really special, and they were. We had a really enjoyable evening. They had the routine down well. We spent much of the evening talking about our hometowns, etc., and whether or not we had a girlfriend back home. Unfortunately for me, all I would think about was Martiel and some of our favorite dance music from our high school days. When the DJ asked for special requests, I requested "Ebb Tide" and "Blue Moon," as sung by Frank Sinatra. Those two songs always reminded me of Fort Lauderdale, especially on weekend nights at the beach (even after I'd spent most of the daytime hours on the *High Hopes* charter fishing boat).

It was during the dance to "Blue Moon" that I first really noticed how much my "date" reminded me of Martiel. What did it was her eyes and how she looked at me. I told her she had beautiful eyes, and she hesitated, looked at me, and said, "You have the most beautiful green eyes I've ever seen." And then, for that one timeless moment, we both just looked into each other's eyes. I was back with Martiel on the beach, and I didn't want to leave. Martiel had said the very same thing to me when we first met. Anyhow, we had a great time that evening after all, and when it was time for the girls to leave, she said she would look for me Saturday morning the following week at graduation. She would be in the middle stands, first seat, first row, with two other girls as our company passed in review. I knew I'd be on the starboard side in our formation, outside first or second row, come hell or high water. Well, I was there, eager and ready to meet her after the ceremony. She wasn't there, and I never heard from her again. But I still have the memory.

We were through with most of our recruit training and testing routine, and on Monday morning we began preparing for our graduation coming up on Saturday, with all the pomp and circumstance, recognition for sports competition and academics, etc., and individual honors. Company 389 was one of the better overall recruit companies at that graduation ceremony, and we got the rest of the day off to visit the commissary to purchase souvenirs, etc., to take back home. We'd be leaving the following Monday, after a final cleaning of our barracks.

The week passed quickly. Monday, after morning chow, we returned to our barracks for the final time to pick up our orders, gather our gear, and finish packing our seabags, exchange home addresses, and say our final goodbyes and good lucks. I listened intently as our company commander called out our names and handed out orders with a handshake.

I had no orders. The only one in the company. When our company commander handed out the last set of orders, he called me aside and told me I'd be sleeping over alone that night and would pick up my orders at recruit command headquarters at 0800 the next morning. Promptly.

For whatever reason, I didn't sleep well that night and felt alone, not knowing what was happening. When I arrived at recruit command headquarters, I was directed to an officer's office. He told me to shut the door; he took a large, well-sealed package from his desk drawer and told me to sit down. He then proceeded to tell me I had been selected for a twenty-six-week classified Naval Intelligence program at the San Diego Recruit Training Command, where I would first undergo an eight-week radio operator class while the Navy completed a background investigation and subsequently granted a top-secret intelligence clearance if I qualified.

Following this action, I would be transferred to Imperial Beach for the final intelligence training program of sixteen weeks. He then told me I had been selected for this billet based on my test scores during the past eight weeks and my high school records. Then I remembered something. In one of the interview sessions a few weeks earlier, the interviewer had told me he was recommending me to strike for the electronics operator ratings. When I said that would be fine with me, he had me sign the enlisted classification record form and then initial it in the box marked "I volunteer for CT duty." That was the first and only time I knew I had volunteered for "CT" duty, whatever that was. All I knew was that the form indicated my billet was CT-2409-85. When I'd asked the guys in my company, I don't recall any of them saying they had to sign and initial their job or school assignment form. The officer then stood up, congratulated me, shook my hand, handed me the package of orders, and told me not to open the package. He then gave me an airline ticket home. As I stood up, I said something to the effect of "Thank you, sir," to which he replied, "Thank you, sailor. You're extremely fortunate. Best of luck to you, and as we say in the Navy, 'May fair winds and following seas go with you.'

So that's the story of boot camp at Naval Station Great Lakes, Navy style. I was on my way, but where I was going, I really didn't know. And I was the only one from my company on this journey. All I really knew was that I knew absolutely nothing about my future in the Navy. I had no clue. Duty here in the U.S.? Shipboard duty? An overseas assignment? Doing what? When I'd first arrived at Great Lakes eight weeks earlier, I'd said to myself, "What have I done?" My thought at this moment was *God help me!* I was alone—again.

That night my flight out of Chicago's Midway Airport was

delayed twice. When I finally did board at 0100 or 0200, I was the only passenger, with the pilot, the co-pilot, and two stewardesses on a deadhead flight to Miami—first class. I was beginning to feel better. Not bad, in fact. I was looking forward to my fourteen-day leave.

When that first leave was over, I was on my way to intel school in California. I had packed some civvies—one or two pairs of pants, a few casual shirts, a light rain jacket, a bathing suit—as well as pictures for the locker, of family and of Martiel.

FOUR

RADIO AND INTELLIGENCE SCHOOLS

M orse code is a method of transmitting a message or other information in the form of a text using, using a series of short and long signals called "dots" and "dashes," which are electronically generated and transmitted over varying radio waves. Each Morse code symbol represents either a text (letter or numeral) or a prosign (SOS, the standard distress signal, is a Morse code prosign) and is represented by a unique sequence of dots and dashes. SOS is transmitted in the format of three dots, three dashes, and three dots. Morse code was extensively used in World War II and the Cold War, primarily by military and governmental agencies. But new advances in communication methods have made it obsolete today as the primary means of sending messages.

Transmitting code—rather than receiving, or copying, code—was the hardest part for me to learn. My wrist had to be totally relaxed so I could create a rhythm of sorts with my sending; it couldn't just be a mechanical movement of my hand. That simple fact is what gives rise to a really competent intercept operator's ability to "identify" the sender of a message, especially in guerrilla situations, where you're constantly attempting to locate the transmitter by frequency equipment as the guerrillas move their location from place to place, nearly constantly changing transmitting frequencies. It became quite simple, for me, to follow an individual transmitter by his transmitting "characteristics"—that is, the rhythm and length of time between elements of a character, the "swing" in the difference between *dit dit dit dah* and *ditditdit dah*, if you get what I mean. It eventually became relatively simple to determine that a certain individual operator had been transferred from Moscow to Odessa just by listening to him transmit.

This often proved to be important, because the USSR generally used their "burst" operators to transmit the most important messages. Accordingly, the Navy tended to use their "best" intercept operators on the most critical operations because of the much improved "end result" of the intercept—i.e., the precision and overall quality of their work.

Four of us were standing around after our final examination at radio school at the Naval Training Center San Diego, Service School Command. We didn't know if there would be a graduation ceremony or not, but we did know the four of us would be leaving for Imperial Beach for the final sixteen weeks of intelligence school. Radio school had been a bitch, with several guys flunking out or dropping back a week during those first eight weeks. They didn't make it, simply because of the constant, eight-hour, daylong stress of attempting to learn how to simultaneously type while listening to and copying Morse code.

The final exam had been a thirty-minute constant stream of listening to and copying Morse code coming at you at roughly fifteen words per minute, which was nearly impossible back then. Once you lost your concentration, it was pretty much over for you. Somehow, perhaps by the grace of God, Ski and I had made it through the radio school and final exam without a major mishap, and we were on our way to Imperial Beach. I had never been so grateful in my life, and it was an experience I'll never forget.[5]

To get through the final exam, you had to concentrate, and I mean *concentrate!* There were near-constant pauses or interruptions in the radio transmissions. For example, a multitude of "Q" signals can signify many different situations: "QSY" means either "Should I change to another frequency?" or "Change to frequency A," depending on whether you initiated the "Q" signal or you received it. Problem was, you had to know the existence of about seventy-five to one hundred of them, along with lists and lists of such abbreviations as "AS" for "Stand by," "IMI" for "Repeat," and so on.

Along with all that confusion, if you hesitated or paused to consider if what you just heard—or thought you heard—was an *L* (·−··) or an *F* (··−·), you'd be lost and probably never recover because the Morse code just kept coming at you furiously fast. So what you needed to do was listen for an entire word instead of an individual letter. You had to stop and start up again with the next group or word set. It was a real son of a bitch to learn, but once you did become proficient in Morse code, you *never* forgot it.

Here's an example: Today, as I write this book, I recall an event that took place about twenty-five years ago (around 1990), before I retired from my banking career. I was playing around with my shortwave radio at home and picked up— loud and clear—a Morse code transmission of coded numeric blocks of five numerals, which ran for close to ten minutes

5. Ski and I first met at the radio school class at the Naval Training Center San Diego. We came from separate boot camps—Ski from the East Coast, I from the Midwest. We would attend sixteen weeks of intelligence school together on the Silver Strand in Imperial Beach. After that, we were paired for the remainder of our Naval service. After our service, Ski eventually moved to Florida, and we attended Florida State University together. We had a bond and a lifelong friendship.

before completing the transmission and signing off. To me, the composition, transmission, and sending was reminiscent of Soviet diplomatic CW (continuous wave) radio transmissions, such as between Moscow and Pyongyang, North Korea, which I had intercepted on Guam in the 1950s. I'd copied about fifty to seventy-five blocks before the message ended.

Later that week, an FBI agent I knew was in the bank, and I mentioned it to him, explaining what I thought it sounded like to me. He asked me if I had a copy of the transmission, which I did. I gave it to him, and he said he'd get back with me. About a month or so later, he stopped by and asked me how I'd come to find and copy the transmission. I told him I'd learned it at Imperial Beach back in the 1950s, when I'd been in Naval intelligence school.

He said, "That explains it."

"Explains what?" I asked.

"The office told me the Navy had moved that school to Pensacola, Florida, a few years back."

What I had copied was a class assignment given to intelligence school students at the Pensacola Naval base. I continued to listen for that transmission site for several weeks, but I didn't find it again and soon gave up. Guess the Navy changed frequencies and/or transmission times, but I'll never know. Nice memories, however.

Back to the radio school story: Ski and I learned that out of the eighteen or so guys who took that final exam, only thirteen had passed. The guys who didn't pass were either dropped back a week or returned to the fleet for reassignment. Over the years I've thought about some of them we knew fairly well, and I wondered how they fared in the Navy.

The day we completed our radio school exam was one of those quintessential San Diego weather days—clear blue skies, cool autumn temperatures—and four of us, dressed in our crisp white summer uniforms, were ready for a mini-adventure. Someone suggested the San Diego Zoo, which we all thought was a good idea. We got a cab at the front gate of the base, and once we arrived, we started down one of the pathways to where the African animals were housed: elephants, rhinos, lions, gorillas, birds, you name it. All at once we came across a huge male gorilla and his mate sitting on quite a large boulder inside a cage, maybe thirty-five by forty-five feet and twelve to fifteen feet high, with heavy steel bars about twelve inches apart across the front of the cage, where visitors passed by. One of the guys we were with had stopped in front of the gorillas' cage, maybe two or three feet away from the bars, and was mocking the male, pretending to be a gorilla. He was whooping and jerking his arms up and down by his sides, while the gorilla was looking at him and moving around anxiously on his perch, making loud noises. Funny sight.

All of a sudden, the gorilla reached down and picked up a large handful of gorilla poop and whipped it with all his might toward our buddy, who by now was nearly touching the bars of the cage. I mean it was a great shot—straight through the opening between the bars and WHAM! right square in the middle of his chest. You could actually hear it hit! THUMP! I mean it was a pile of poop, bigger than just a small handful, right onto his breastbone, splattering up into his upper chest and down to the belt area of his nice, clean dress whites. All of a sudden, a tremendous "WHAT THE HOLY HELL!" "JESUS CHRIST!" and "*#@!" The gorilla hollered back with a huge roar! At that instant, the other three of us were absolutely flabbergasted! The few other visitors around started laughing hysterically, which only got us going even more. Our buddy was having an absolute fit—tearing at his jumper, trying to get it over his head without spreading the poop all over his hands and hair. We all knew those Navy jumpers would cause us a problem someday, either in a fight or here in a zoo with a ton of gorilla poop all over your chest! With all the laughter and whooping of the gorilla and the carryings-on, two park attendants appeared and they, too, were mortified. That gorilla had never done anything like this before!

About this time, two Navy shore patrol guys, with their nightsticks drawn, also appeared. "What in the hell is going on here, sailors?" one shouted. "Get away from there, now!" I guess they thought we were attacking or harassing or provoking the gorillas. Then they saw our buddy, still trying to figure out how to get his jumper off over his head. Once they saw that, they started laughing as well. Well, after another ten or so zoo visitors came our way and started laughing, things began to die down. The SPs cut his jumper off of him, removed it gingerly, and took him off, I guess back to the Naval base, probably laughing all the way. Bet they couldn't have been happy with the smell in the shore patrol van, though. About that time, some little boy turned and asked his mom, "Mom, what was that man doing?" More laughter.

After our buddy left with the SPs, we continued on our way around the zoo, had a great lunch, and kept laughing and rehashing what we'd just witnessed. And it was a long time before we stopped talking and laughing about the entire experience. Then we were in a cab back to the Naval base and getting ready for the trip to Imperial Beach in the morning and our final sixteen weeks of intelligence school. I think it was nearly a week before our buddy would even speak to us. He was still too embarrassed about the "Incident at the Zoo."

Once we arrived at the main administration building on the base at Imperial Beach the next morning, located right on the Pacific Ocean, we got off the bus, walked through the gated area, and moved our gear into the nearby barracks. We noticed there were no buildings taller than one story, and there were literally thirty or forty various antenna arrays in the immediate area. There were the admin building, a group of smaller buildings, the chow hall, the chapel, the library, etc.—and classroom buildings around a main auditorium.

After we came out of our barracks, we were told to get over to the main auditorium for our "Welcome Aboard" speech and introduction to the school. We were told what the requirements were, grade performance expectations, the course of instruction—all the same-old, same-old of any school environment. There were about forty or fifty of us, I guessed from all over the country, including some Marines, all here for the same purpose. Whatever that really was. Right away we were told that our class designation was 13-D-56 and our instructor was Chief Petty Officer Wright.

Two senior-level officers, probably a lieutenant commander and a full commander, in dress blues, entered and took center stage. After a very brief introduction to Imperial Beach and our school, they got right to the point. We were special. We were privileged. We were the best of the Navy's latest "recruits," and we'd already proven ourselves in our performance in boot camp and in our initial radio training course. We were on our way to becoming full members of the Navy's signals intelligence (SIGINT) section. We would soon be Navy *cryptologists*. With top-secret military clearances from the chief of naval operations.

Then the commander gave us our first introduction to just what we would undergo for the next sixteen weeks, a time when all of us would be subject to intensive background investigations by national organizations—looking into our moral and personal background as well as that of our family, friends, and associates—before receiving our final clearance.

He started by saying that though the Navy had used Morse and other codes and ciphers since 1775, it wasn't until the advent of electronic radio communications that they had become essential to successful operations. And it wasn't until the early 1900s that the Navy began systematic efforts to ensure that its communications were secure and that it had the capability to exploit the communications of our enemies.

In the 1920s the Navy formally established a cryptologic

component, known as OP-20-G (in our time the component was known as OP-30-G), which recognized that the future of cryptology lay in machine cipher systems rather than in manually operated strip ciphers, which had remained significantly unchanged since the late 1700s. Coupled with these efforts was the utilization of linguist specialists, who in the 1940s had been responsible for initially translating the Japanese Navy code during World War II.

World War II had demonstrated the absolute need for centralized management of SIGINT—signals intelligence—and the trend toward increasingly complex technology and more extraordinarily sophisticated equipment continued. This culminated in the establishment of the Naval Security Group (OP-30-G) in 1950 and the National Security Agency in 1952 by an act of Congress.

Since the end of World War II, the Naval Security Group has continued to support the signals intelligence effort in war, in operations other than war, and during dangerous periods in peacetime, including the monitoring of guerrilla and rogue nations that operated in various regions of the world. The move of the NSA in the late 1950s and of the NSG's headquarters in 1996 to Fort George G. Meade, outside of Washington, D.C., brought even closer the relationship between the NSG and the NSA. While the end of the Soviet Empire, on December 26, 1991, has changed the world entirely, that world still remains a dangerous place for humanity as a whole. The need for signals intelligence to support the fleet and the nation continues. The U.S. Navy and its officers and enlisted men remain dedicated to that effort. The commander's introductory talk had a shocking and profound impact on all of us.

Of interest to me and some others in our class that first week was the fact that the small town of Imperial Beach was one of Southern California's premier surfing beaches. It had an excellent bathing beach and a pier about 150 yards long, as well as an almost ideal shoreline for surfing. Believe it or not, I was the only one in our Basic Intelligence class who knew anything about surfing—and that wasn't much.

Back in Fort Lauderdale during high school, I'd had a touch of experience the winter of 1953, when the area experienced more than a few "nor'easters," as we called them, which brought the area some relatively good waves for surfing. Over a two-to-three-week period, one of the guys picked up a surfboard somewhere. It was about nine feet long—a so-called long board in those days. Truthfully, it was all I could do to stand up for probably not more than a minute or two before coming off the board entirely. It wasn't anything to do with the weight of the board; it was made of balsa—so said the guy who owned it. It was simply the fact that I had no idea of what I was doing—and still don't, although I greatly admire the sport.

At Imperial Beach, what several of us in the class would do was go down, generally on Saturday morning, and watch the guys surf. The waves in this area were usually in the range of eight to ten feet—sometimes higher, but that was only during times when the surf was really up, way above the regular surf at that beach. That's where we learned how surfers know when to make an appearance at certain beaches along the California coast. We were amazed, to say the least. Back in Fort Lauderdale during the winter of 1953, we knew about the waves simply because one of us (didn't matter who) called and said the surf was up. These guys at Imperial Beach had taken that to a much higher level.

Many California beaches are noted for their surfing conditions. Imperial Beach was one of them. A major player, to say the least. The weekend before, there probably weren't more than one or two guys who appeared on the beach, and no one was in the water except the bathers and small children. Today, just one week later, no one was in the water with the exception of maybe a dozen surfers at 0800. Here's why: About Monday or Tuesday of that week, the locals (including guys from San Diego and the surrounding areas) started the search for weather and sea conditions in the Aleutian Islands and the Bering Sea by getting the reports of the U.S. Geological Survey and the local weather bureau for their forecasts on winds, seas, and wave model projections to help the surfers create wave models and tide conditions in the Southern California area over the next few days. And they were virtually always right on the money.

On Thursday, for example, waves in the area had been roughly four-to-five-footers, but by Saturday morning, the wave heights and swells were in the twelve-to-fifteen-foot range, and there was no way I was going to get out in that surf! This might be the only time in my life I'd ever be called a "pansy," but it didn't bother me a bit. These guys showed up on Saturday morning simply because they had read the tide and weather conditions in Alaska earlier in the week and knew what to expect. Plain and simple. Everyone else saw the tides and got off the beach! We watched these surfers for hours.

My cousin Lindy's oldest son, Mike Redela, grew up surfing these West Coast waves by checking weather reports daily and grabbing his surfboard to catch a wave when the conditions were just right—and still making it to school before the first-period bell rang! He's a family man now, teaching his children the freedom and serenity of "soul surfing" in the San Diego waves—not far from where these locals surfed sixty years ago.

Then there was another notable event. One day, after class and chow, a group of us went down to the beach area in front of the base administration office, just to sit around and enjoy the evening. We'd been there maybe an hour or two and it had just gotten somewhat dark, when one of the guys yelled out, "What the hell is that in the water?" We all started looking about, expecting anything from flotsam or a shark or something along those lines, when a guy stood up in the surf and walked ashore. "Jesus, what the hell?" It was a frogman. He was fully dressed in a black wet suit, flippers, full face mask, and snorkel. He was in training at the Naval Training Center San Diego frogman school and was at the point in his training when he had to make an unaccompanied swim from two miles or so out in the Pacific Ocean on a dark night to shore, using the stars and a compass only. This was not like a swim in the pool; it was in an environment of seas four to five feet, and ground swells even higher. To our surprise, he was followed a few moments later by another frogman and then another. Three guys, dropped off by boat two miles at sea on a dark night, unaccompanied, and told to head for Imperial Beach as their "shore point" to complete a critical student frogman test. *Christ,* I thought, *what the hell am I doing in the Navy? I need to get out of here.* Still shakes me to think about that night. We talked about it for a long time, even searching the waters at night, after chow, until we forgot about it several weeks later. We never saw any frogmen again.

Our first day of class was interesting, to say the least— more of a shock than anything else. Our instructor told us that in addition to learning the history of the NSG and its relationship to the NSA in Washington, D.C., we would be spending a considerable amount of time studying the history of radio communications and SIGINT, principally relating to Nazi Germany and the Allies during World War II up to today and the Cold War. Yes, it was a complete shock to all thirty of us in the room. So that's why we had spent eight weeks at the Naval Training Center in San Diego, learning how to type and, most importantly, how to send and receive CW Morse code at a basic level!

The first thing our instructor did was give each of us a copy of a book titled *War Secrets in the Ether* by Wilhelm F. Flicke, a German SIGINT operative. This book had initially been published in 1947 in Germany after the war. Upon publication, the U.S. government, so the story goes, purchased all copies and banned their sale in the U.S. And here we had a copy for our reading over the next eight weeks. Nice job, Navy. Our instructor told us that for the next eight weeks, we'd be using this book as a historical and "technical" textbook for background purposes in our study of SIGINT and its related equipment, specifically all the current electronics, including radio transmitters/receivers, direction-finding equipment, and a multitude of Naval communications antenna arrays. We soon found out, however, that the bulk of our studies would center upon learning and working with a variety of real-time equipment as part of our job. And that was an incredibly challenging task for all of us.

What follows is our instructor's short summary of what, to us, was the most stunning part of the book, simply because it involved German Field Marshal Erwin Rommel, one of the greatest and best-known generals of the World War II German Army. There wasn't one of us in the class who hadn't heard of him for what we all previously had believed was his military genius. Historians generally agree that Field Marshal Rommel was the ultimate symbol of leadership, military skill, and tactical ability, especially for his campaigns in the Sahara Desert of North Africa from 1941 to 1943. He and his Afrika Korps troops won astonishing victories time and time again and nearly pushed the British out of the African campaign in battles against British Field Marshal Bernard Montgomery and General Archibald Wavell among others.

Before Rommel appeared in Africa in 1941, General Wavell had been successful in offensives against Germany's Italian allies when they pushed across the Egyptian border and proceeded westward in a major advance in December 1940. By mid-March 1941, General Wavell had driven the Italians back to the borders of Tripoli. It was at this point that the Afrika Korps, led by Rommel, started a major offensive against Wavell.

What happened next was to become one of the most significant events in the history of the German African campaign
and the Allies' war with Germany. It changed the history of
the war and brought to light the incredible impact of wartime
SIGINT and "secrets in the ether" and the impact of German
intelligence agencies on the conduct of modern warfare. Our
instructor then virtually slapped us in the face as he related
this story. A U.S. military attaché, Colonel Bonner Fellers, stationed in Cairo, had been sending encrypted radio
transmissions to Washington on an almost daily basis.
Although encrypted, and relatively secure, they had been
intercepted by German intelligence operatives who noticed
something unique about them. They all bore the same cover
name and address, "*agwr wash*," which equated to "Adjunct
General, War Department, Washington, D.C." Therefore, they
were easily recognized, even though they were encrypted.

However, the death knell of any encrypted system is found
in its frequency of usage. As a result, by the spring of 1941,
German intelligence had succeeded in breaking much of the
encoded messages. And what the Germans uncovered turned
out to be of astounding significance to the German war effort
in Africa, especially for Rommel. Fellers was regularly sending encrypted radio transmissions to Washington, reporting
to the War Department detailed information regarding rein-
forcement of British troops in Egypt; comments regarding
their equipment, including when transportation of various
war materials arrived and where; information regarding the
withdrawal of Australian Ninth Division troops from Tobruk
and their replacement by British units; and significant information regarding preparation for offensive actions against
various German troop movements, especially those under
Rommel. All the intercepted and decoded messages were
passed immediately to Rommel, who planned his movements
accordingly.

By late summer 1941, most British actions against Rommel

were failing in some degree or another. When the British generals attacked Rommel's position, he would immediately send forces to oppose them as they appeared at the battle sites, or even before they appeared at the battle site, he would send a column of tanks behind the British forces, breaking their connections. Many have commented that Rommel always seemed to do the right thing at the right time.

Unknown to the Allies, German intercept stations intensified their efforts to intercept and transmit the attaché's messages as soon as possible and teletype them to Berlin, where they were deciphered and forwarded to Rommel, many times as quickly as a few hours after the messages' initial receipt. By almost complete access to the military plans of the British, Rommel was able to break their battle plans at will. For example, in the Battle of Sidi Rezegh, the German garrison at Halfaya Pass was able to hold its position and force the British to transport critically needed supplies and equipment across the desert. Rommel began regrouping his troops and escaped without being detected before the British discovered he was gone.

In January 1942, Rommel advanced deep into the British line near El Agheila with three armored columns, taking the British by surprise and forcing them again to retreat. A few days later, on January 27, he was just north of Maus. On that day, Winston Churchill declared, "We are facing a very bold and clever foe, and I may well say, a great general." On January 29 Rommel took Benghazi. The British operations in North Africa were rapidly falling apart. So important was the intercepted information Rommel continued to receive that Berlin ordered him, after receiving substantial reinforcements and supplies, to drive his forces to the Suez Canal, where he was ordered to go beyond Jerusalem and Damascus into northern Arabia and Iraq to join forces with the troops recently withdrawn from Russia. It appeared to the Allies that the days of British dominance in the Near East were now numbered and the British lifeline through the Mediterranean and the Red Sea was about to be cut.

Finished with his summary, our instructor said one final remark before moving on to the day's other business. He said that during World War II, 6 million Americans served in the armed forces, 200,000 of whom died. Without the intelligence community, an additional 400,000 or more would have died.

Around noon on Friday, February 3, 1956, we'd finished the basic CT-R coursework. Before dismissal for the weekend, Chief Petty Officer Wright shut down the various radio and electronics equipment we'd been studying and training on for the past eight weeks. He turned off the overhead lights in the room and sat down on the edge of his desk, looked out at us, and said some words of wisdom. "I am proud of each of you sailors. We started this Basic Intelligence class eight weeks ago with thirty students. Some of you were still struggling with Morse code from radio school in San Diego, others with the technical aspects of the various equipment during that time. You'll get it right and be fully competent by the end of the Advanced Intelligence class over the next eight weeks. A few of you may not receive your final top-secret clearance and will leave here for another post in the Navy. And a few of you may not make it through the final eight weeks of this twenty-four-week course for one reason or another."

He went on to say, "But whatever your final situation, you should be proud of what you have accomplished. Many of you are only eight weeks from graduating from one of the hardest schools the Navy has to offer. It is a highly complex and technical billet—extremely challenging and demanding— one you will be proud of all your life, whether you make the Navy your career or move on with other aspects of your life. At this juncture, we're down from thirty to nineteen original class members. About normal for a group of this nature. Monday morning at 0800, we'll meet in the main auditorium. There you will be met by a representative from the NSA and the commanding officer, NSG, of this command. You will be told more about the NSA, about the NSG, and what your specific group mission will be. I'm told you will also be informed about the status of your final security clearance."

Finally, Chief Petty Officer Wright ended with the following: "When you complete the Advanced Intelligence class in eight weeks, you'll be assigned to your first duty station, generally for a tour of eighteen months, after which you will be reassigned to a second duty station for the balance of your enlistment or return to your reserve unit, as applicable. Your initial assignment will normally be an overseas or a shipboard assignment anywhere in the world. Again, congratulations to you all. Dis-*missed.*"

One of the first things we noticed when we entered Chief Petty Officer Rice's Advanced Intelligence class was something printed on the blackboard above his desk. He pointed it out and asked if any of us in the class knew what it was and what it said.

It was kind of quiet in the class. Then one guy said, "Looks like Latin to me."

"That's right," Chief Rice said. "What's it say?"

Nobody said a word.

"Good. I didn't expect you would know. I will tell you this much, though. It's not much different from the same thing SIGINT says about CW Morse code—especially Soviet CW Morse code. I'd suggest you pick one of you to go to the base library tonight and see what you can find. Then we'll discuss it tomorrow."

Well, what was on the board over his desk was (I hope) this:

"Quidquid latine dictum sit, altum sonatur."

[Translation: "Whatever is said in Latin sounds profound."]

We finally did come up with the translation, after which Chief Petty Officer Rice proceeded to explain that a live Soviet encrypted coded message transmitted by CW Morse code is just about as complex and complicated as SIGINT can be. It's profound. "Don't think for a minute that the Morse code you learned in radio school and the Beginning Intelligence class here at Imperial Beach is anywhere near as indicative of what you'll be faced with in the future. And it begins *now*."

With that, he turned on a tape cassette and exposed us to the real environment and sound of an actual Soviet diplomatic CW radio transmission between Moscow and one of its diplomatic posts somewhere in the world. Believe me, it was so startling and confusing to hear and comprehend what it was that none of us could speak. And the reality was, we didn't get over it until several weeks into the class.

Chief Petty Officer Rice gave basically the same speech as the one we had received from Chief Petty Officer Wright when we'd graduated from Basic Intelligence in February. It was early May 1956, and it had been one hell of a final eight weeks, starting with an introduction to our future with the NSG and the NSA and the disclosure that our job would entail SIGINT gathering against the USSR throughout the world, with a concentration on Soviet submarine fleet operations and diplomatic communications between Moscow and all its consulate offices around the world.

Some of us might also be involved with guerrilla-type SIGINT in various countries around the world. Ski and I had been paired up and were on our way to Guam for an eighteen-month tour of duty at the Naval Communications Station, Finegayan Beach.

We left the classroom feeling good, to say the least. Here we were, done after an extensive twenty-four-week training program and looking at an overseas assignment as an electronics intelligence operative with the NSG. Some of us would go solo, while others would be paired off, as Ski and I had been, with various top-secret duties and assignments. I felt good—as good as I'd ever felt in my life. I was especially proud at that moment of my cryptographic security clearance and that I would be working for one of the best intelligence agencies in the world. Who's lucky enough to get that assignment and responsibility? At age seventeen?

We said our goodbyes, and each of us knew the chances were that we'd never see each other again, certainly not as a group. All I did know for certain was that Ski and I would be paired as "brothers" and serve our first tour together on Guam—where twelve years earlier, almost to the day, my uncle John had served during World War II as a captain in the Marine Corps during the invasion of Guam at Apra Harbor in 1944.

Of course, it could be only a coincidence that Ski and I had met at a San Diego training facility just as my uncle John had met his Marine buddy Chuck at Camp Elliott in San Diego in 1943. Chuck Zell (a "brother" to my uncle John) was also from Pennsylvania, served with my uncle on Guam, and later was with him when he was wounded on Iwo Jima. It was Chuck who summoned the jeep that took my uncle to the beach, where an infusion of whole blood (which had arrived that very morning) saved his life.

I choose to believe that the same warrior ancestors who protected Uncle John on Iwo were also watching me around the same time, as I fished off the docks in Old Lyme, knowing I would soon need a "brother," as Uncle John did. Divine orchestration or random chance? You decide.

Back to the barracks to pick up our orders and papers, seabag and other gear, and head out to the San Diego Airport for the long flight home and a two-week leave. Guam was a long way away.

FIVE

GUAM AND THE MARIANA ISLANDS

The Mariana Islands are a crescent-shaped archipelago comprising the summits of fifteen mostly dormant volcanic mountains. The islands are located in the western Pacific Ocean, the main island of which is Guam. In 1956, Guam was a paradise on earth to any sailor who had never experienced such a life. Despite growing up in Fort Lauderdale, I was absolutely thrilled and thankful for my first tour of duty in a place such as this.

The capital of Guam today is Hagåtña, known in English in the mid-1950s as "Agana." It is a beautiful small town, located on the central shore of the Pacific Ocean at Agana Harbor, site of one of two U.S. military invasions in World War II and where we used to go snorkeling for "artifacts," in spite of a Navy posting on the beach warning: "Removal of any U.S. Naval Artifacts will result in Court-Martial Proceedings."

The other invasion site was Apra Harbor, which was the current site of the U.S. Naval base, approximately twelve miles southwest of Agana Harbor. This is where I went aboard a submarine for temporary duty assignment (TDA) shortly after the launch of *Sputnik* by the USSR in October 1957.

Tumon, and Tumon Bay, northeast of Agana, was a small

village in the 1950s, but it was once one of the most prominent villages in precolonial Guam; it is presently the principal
Japanese tourist center—thick with foreign-owned hotels,
bars and nightclubs, restaurants, duty-free shopping sites,
strip clubs, massage parlors, and gun shops. In essence,
since the mid-1950s, it has become fully "Americanized." To
pave the way for the tourist industry that has taken over a
onetime true "paradise," large sections of coral reefs in the
bay and along the shoreline that were there during the war
years and mid-1950s, when Ski and I were there, were
destroyed. In addition, massive mechanized sand sweeping
that contributed heavily to soil erosion, growing amounts of
sewage runoff, and the use of motorized water recreational
vehicles have nearly destroyed much of the fish population
and other water life on the reefs and other areas of the bay.
But in spite of all this development over the years since we
were there, it appears that the Chamorro people of Guam
have survived the constantly moving and changing islands
that make up the Marianas, including Guam. I hope that is
still true.

The Naval Security Group's Naval Communications Station, Finegayan Beach, Guam, was established in 1954. It was
an NSG intelligence base that principally operated secret
high-frequency direction-finding (HF/DF) antenna arrays
located in aboveground and underground offices in the center
of an AN/FRD-10A circularly disposed antenna array (CDAA,
known as a Wullenweber, or "elephant cage") from 1957 to
1999. That antenna array still remains, unused, on the site of
the Naval Computer and Telecommunications Station (NCTS,
or NAVCOMTELSTA), Guam. It was constructed shortly after
the launch of *Sputnik*, and "burst" radio communications were
developed by the USSR around the time of that launch. The
base was part of the Pacific Net of HF/DF submarine and surface detection systems, an integral element of the Navy's ASW
(anti-submarine warfare) program.

We arrived at Andersen Air Force Base, on the northern-most point of Guam, by way of a Military Air Transport Service (MATS) flight from Hawaii to Kwajalein Atoll in the Marshall Islands, approximately 2,200 miles southwest of Hawaii, and then on to Guam. Kwajalein is one of the smallest inhabited islands in the Pacific, populated mostly by a thousand or so American military personnel and located some 1,600 miles southeast of Guam. All in all, the mileage from Fort Lauder-dale to Guam was roughly 9,000 miles, which to me was one hell of a long way, even though all of it was by air. Matter of fact, it sure beat the return trip to the U.S. in 1957, which was by ship (the USS *Virgo*) and took twenty-two days.

After a twenty-minute ride on a Navy bus from Andersen Air Force Base, we arrived at the entrance to the Naval Com-munications Station, Finegayan Beach. As we drove through the gate area and up the slight hill (which obscured the inside of the base), there was the beginning of a remarkable view of the northern portion of the island of Guam. We were on the crest of the second-highest ridgeline on Guam and could see from that end of the island to nearly halfway to the other end, with the expanse of the Pacific Ocean on both sides of us in the distance. A high plateau stretched off to the north, beyond Finegayan Beach, to the area around Andersen Air Force Base. The ridgeline wound its way south across the highest peak on Guam, Mount Tenjo, and dropped off to the Pacific Ocean beyond the capital, Agana, and near Apra Harbor and the present U.S. Naval base.

It was a place of unusual beauty, to say the least, and one we were to call "home" for the next eighteen months. At the very spot where our intelligence base was constructed, a fierce battle with the Japanese Army had taken place with the U.S. Marines, and abundant evidence of that battle, such as Japanese tanks and mortars, was still being discovered in the pineapple fields and in the caves on the cliffs overlooking the beaches and coves. The views were beautiful. Being on the western shore of the island, we could enjoy the sight of the setting sun almost every night.

We soon located our favorite beach among the many in the area, one with a small cove and barrier reef that kept the surf relatively calm around the sandy beach, which was overgrown with coconut palms, rooted from coconuts that floated ashore almost daily. When Ski and I weren't on daytime duty, we'd usually head for that beach with pineapples from the local fields, a six-pack or two of San Miguel Beer, a machete to open the coconuts we harvested from the palms growing on the beach, and a fishing rod to catch a meal. Depending on whether or not we had an "EVE watch" that afternoon, we were set for the day! Daily life by the sea was an exquisite pleasure we could never have expected back when we joined the Navy, and we spent many hours at that little beach paradise on Guam.

The time had passed quickly since our arrival on Guam a week earlier. Ski and I got up this particular morning, knowing that we were beginning our two-week orientation that day. We were looking forward to it, but we couldn't really understand why we needed another two weeks for orientation. We'd been sitting around for nearly a week and were more than ready to go. We soon got a rude awakening. Thinking about it while lying around the barracks during the preceding week, we knew that soon we would be putting to work all we had learned those previous sixteen weeks at Imperial Beach. Now here we were, on Guam, five thousand miles from California, on the front lines of the Cold War. Now, after all those weeks of learning the ropes, we were going "live." This was real. The Cold War was, in hindsight, a battlefield with no weapons, soldiers, or sailors, but it was something just as important. When we sat down at our job, it would be like being in a room looking over the shoulders of presidents, government officials, generals, and admirals who were developing battlefield plans, new weapons, and all the aspects of war. When they had discussions with their field generals and troops, we'd be preparing what we'd observed from their meeting, for our men to develop counterplans and weapons to defeat the enemies of our country. How important is that? Ask Churchill or Rommel or Patton how important it was. And to us, we were the most important element—the critical cog—the intelligence community, the hunters and gatherers of knowledge about the enemy, the war secrets in the ether. We were the Navy's Cold War warriors. And we were proud of it.

The main Ops Center (Receiver) was Building 150, away from the barracks, Base Administration, and chow hall area of the base about a half mile up an unpaved road. It was the NSG receiver site (our duty site), located at the edge of a large antenna field with a series of long rhombic antennae. The antennae were directed toward various target locations throughout the Pacific, including Vladivostok, Russia, the USSR's primary Pacific Ocean submarine base, located at the southern end of the Muravyov-Amursky Peninsula. It borders China and North Korea. The NSG transmitter site, Barrigada, was located approximately twelve miles to the southwest of our base.

The rhombic antenna was a broadband directional wire antenna, mostly used in the high-frequency (HF) or short-wave CW Morse code bands. It usually consists of three parallel wires suspended above the ground in a "rhombic" (diamond) pattern, supported by poles at each vertex, to which the wires are attached by insulators. Its principal advantage over other types of antennae is its simplicity. It has a wide bandwidth and the ability to operate over a wide range of frequencies. Such an antenna requires a large area of land, especially if several antennae are installed to serve a variety of geographic regions at different distances or directions and to cover widely different frequencies. During World War II, and afterward until the late 1950s, it was one of the most used point-to-point high-frequency antenna arrays. In the Navy it was replaced in the late 1950s and early 1960s by the AN/FRD-10 CDAA "elephant cage," developed for the primary purpose of determining the location and direction of Soviet "burst" submarine CW radio transmissions.

So we got on the bus, rode for a few minutes to Building 150. We passed through the Marine guard and stopped at what we knew to be the operations center. At the entrance door to the working area there, an armed Marine guard checked to see that each of us displayed the proper ID tag, which had to be worn at all times inside the building. After we passed through the first door, there was a second door that required a security code to enter. Once we were inside this area, there were several other areas that also required security codes to open the door (in addition to an ID tag that was color coded to permit entrance). Since none of us had ever been in the building before, there was an officer who accompanied us once the Marine at the front entrance had verified our access authority.

At approximately 0800, we stepped inside what would be our working quarters for the next seventeen months. This was the central intercept operations (watch center) area of the building. *God almighty, look at that equipment! That's what it looks like?* Cubicle after cubicle, floor to eight feet high. Must have been thirty cubicles here. Two desks in the center of the room, occupied by two officers. *Whoa!* All but maybe two or three of the thirty-some cubicles were occupied. Guys just like us. Two guys walking around the room, collecting work product from each cubicle. *God, this is real!* And what was that guy on the bus saying about work schedules? Three eight-hour watch periods? First, we'd go on the EVE watch, from 1600 to 2400. Then tomorrow, DAY watch from 0800 to 1600, followed by the MID watch from 0000 (2400) to 0800, and then be off the next sixty hours. No Monday-to-Friday, nine-to-five, with the weekend off! Not in the Navy. Four years of this? What kind of job was this, anyway? Welcome to Naval Intelligence, mate.

Each intercept cubicle was equipped with a three-way built-in set of cabinets and shelves containing manual and electronic communication devices, typewriters, volumes of frequency tables, and foreign-country radio call-sign books and manuals. Central to the space was the Collins R-390A military shortwave radio receiver and "mill" (a Royal manual typewriter with a Russian Cyrillic keyboard). My Collins was a double- and triple-conversion superheterodyne receiver, manufactured from 1950 to 1959; it used a mechanical digital dial and supported AM and CW communication modes. It had thirty-two bands of 1-MHz bandwidth, each covering from 0.5 to 32 MHz, and it had thirty-two tubes plus one semiconductor diode. Filtering was made with crystal and cascaded LC filters at 455 KHz and four mechanicals (for 2-, 4-, 8-, and 16-KHz bandwidths). My R-390A was updated from the R-390/URR model. I would be operating similar equipment aboard the submarine when on temporary duty assignment (TDA). In North Africa, I would have the same R-390A, as well as a field model for use in the desert.

Typewriter paper for my Royal was three-copy, continuous sheets, 8x10 formatted. There was a comfortable navy gray leather chair set in front of the mill. At the center of the room was the watch center station, and at one end of the room was a teletype section. Four offices were on the perimeter of the room, housing various CT operatives (CT-Ls, -Ms, -Cs, and -Ts). By far the prevailing noise in the room was the sound of the thirty or more manual typewriters, all of which appeared to be copying CW Morse code transmissions.

I was soon assigned to a CT-R operative, who, after welcoming me aboard, pointed out the two most important elements of the cubicle: the buzzer to the watch center station and the second headphone jack for my use and my evaluator's use. For CW Morse code operatives like me, an evaluator was a junior-grade Naval officer (an ensign or lieutenant junior grade), usually a college-graduate linguist trained at the Defense Language Institute in Monterey, California. That school taught over thirty languages, including Arabic, Chinese, Hindi, Farsi, and Russian among many others, generally over a twenty-four-to-sixty-four-week period, after which time the student was fully qualified for reading, writing, and communicating in one or more of the languages—and many had learned more than one.

Before Ski and I could begin our official duties as CT-Rs, we had to complete this orientation session. It included sitting down with an experienced Morse code intercept operative, working eight-hour shifts on an EVE-watch, a DAY-watch, and a MID-watch schedule over three days, followed by an identical schedule over the ensuing three days alone. In other words, after just three sessions, we'd go "live" for the next seventeen months! The last month of our tour of duty would then include a similar indoctrination session for our replacement, but only if he was a new "first duty station" operative. Similar orientation periods were held for the guys who weren't classified as CT-Rs.

Let me explain something else. At the height of the Cold War (1955–1965), the CT rating was divided into four branches: CT-A, which performed administrative duties; CT-M, responsible for maintaining equipment; CT-O, which were essentially communicators; and CT-R, which were cryptologic radio men. In the 1960s, the CT rating added two additional branches: CT-I, for intercept language work; and CT-T, for non-Morse intercept and the operating of technical equipment.[6] All branches were equally important, but it was well known, to

---

6. Source: "Silent Warriors: The Naval Security Group Reserve, 1945–2005." Publication available from Center for Cryptologic History, National Security Agency, 9800 Savage Road, Suite 6886, Fort George G. Meade, MD 20755-6886.

us at least, that the -R branches were the cream of the crop, the hunters and gatherers of the intelligence community. We were the operatives who had to search for and find the transmitters of highly secretive and sensitive materials and information concerning "war secrets in the ether," copy it accurately, and forward it to the cryptologists and others in Washington for decryption, analysis, and final delivery to the highest governmental and military authorities in the U.S. for their ultimate action.

So, what is all this SIGINT stuff anyway? During our schooling, we were hammered with the idea that the conduct and even the concept of "war" had been forever changed as a result of World War II, that that war had been the beginning of a complete revolution in intelligence and intelligence gathering, and that the impact of intelligence on war strategy, tactics, and the ultimate outcome for both the Allies and Nazi Germany was truly revolutionary.

Today virtually every intelligence agency of every country around the world acknowledges that no other event, including the two atom bombs dropped on Japan late in the war, had such a stunning impact on the conduct of war than SIGINT. Its influence was so pervasive that today it is hard to imagine how the U.S. and its allies might have fought the war without it. Even prior to the actual engagement of U.S. and British forces against the Germans and Japanese, our enemies' two most complex ciphers had been broken and compromised by U.S. and British SIGINT operatives.

The British intelligence efforts at Bletchley Park first produced plaintext reports from the German Enigma submarine communications system in September 1940, while at the same time a U.S. Army group of intelligence operatives successfully broke the Japanese diplomatic cipher machine called Purple, and by 1942, the U.S. Navy intelligence group had broken the Japanese fleet operational code, identified as JN-25. When combined with intelligence successes in cryptology that revealed secrets of direction finding, traffic analysis, and the overall exploitation of plaintext and decrypted communications, SIGINT yielded the Allies an incredible amount of information regarding the conduct of war on the land, on the sea, and in the skies.

In the cipher section of OP-20-G (the 1940s forerunner to the NSA and the NSG) and British intelligence, a grouping of operatives had been set up with excellent technical equipment for monitoring virtually all CW radio transmissions intended for military circles and the highest governmental levels. Hundreds upon hundreds of messages were intercepted daily, evaluated, and categorized. When thoroughly and intensely reviewed, they were a gold mine of information on the armament and troop movement situation in enemy countries. The information derived by the activities of these operatives was of major use to the U.S. in the battle for sea lanes in the Pacific as well. The Japanese merchant marine was nearly completely destroyed because its ship movements were known beforehand, enabling U.S. submarines and surface ships to nearly completely destroy these defenseless and slow-moving merchant vessels plying the western Pacific. In the Atlantic, the U.S. and British used encrypted Enigma messages to track German submarines (U-boats) and to drive their wolf packs from virtually all the sea lanes between England and the continental U.S.

I sat down next to the operative. He plugged in a set of headphones and handed it to me. I put the phones on and almost freaked out. I was listening as my cubicle mate copied—and I'll remember this until I die—Soviet diplomatic code between Moscow and Pyongyang, North Korea. The code was in alpha-block format, five-character Cyrillic blocks transmitted at roughly thirty-five to forty words per minute. I was absolutely blown away. This was real. A Russian CW radio operative, located in Moscow, was transmitting secret information to the Russian embassy (or consulate office) in

Pyongyang, North Korea, just three years after the Korean War! God only knows what information was included in that encrypted message. But the guy sitting next to me had copied it, forwarded it to the appropriate officer for transmission to Washington, to be decrypted and delivered to the appropriate military or governmental official and discussed, as applicable— probably sooner than the intended recipient in North Korea had even read the message!

This was unreal. It was nothing like what we had done in classes back in Imperial Beach. The guy sitting next to me right now had worked his way through static, signal bleeding, signal-strength variances, constant interruptions between sender and receiver, and changes in the composition and structure of the transmission followed by silence. And my cubicle mate might do a frantic search to locate the new frequency, identify it, and commence copying once again. And all this had gone on for what seemed like hours, although in reality it was probably only ten to fifteen minutes before one message was completed and another began, followed by a QSL (receipt confirmation) and maybe another frequency change by the transmitter. My very first experience, and I was completely astonished. I had no idea how I was ever going to do this job. I knew one thing for certain: This was for real, and it was unbelievably complex. No amount of schooling would ever change that fact. Only experience!

This was SIGINT. And for the first time since I'd joined the Navy nearly a year earlier, I was fully aware of the extreme significance of the job I was about to undertake. I knew CT-R branches were known as "hunters and gatherers." What did that really mean? It came to me. At just seventeen, I was a U.S. Navy signals intelligence operative with a top-secret military clearance. I was a *spy*!

First chance the operative had, once he'd finished copying the intercepted message, he told me that we had to maintain a continuous monitoring watch list every ten minutes we were

not copying code. When we were actively working the frequencies, we had to listen continuously for activity on our
assigned target stations. There was no "set in stone" timetable
for the generation and transmission of CW radio traffic from
transmitting station to receiving station that we could rely
upon. This meant that we had to listen to each *dah* and each
dit man-made or natural interference and other "sounds" on
the bands, as well as attempt to detect and discern weak and
barely perceptible transmissions from virtually anyone or
anywhere within our frequency range. Jesus! Then he really
laid it out. He said that the last message he had just finished
copying was transmitted at around thirty-five to forty words
per minute, just a bit above the average for a "Russki." Fine, I
guess, I said to myself. Then he said that high-speed copy
proficiency in CW Morse code was the number-one goal of an
intercept operative. That meant me. If I wanted to be copying
during critical or peak radio traffic periods, I'd better be good,
which meant a minimum of thirty-five to forty words per minute. Only the most skilled CW Morse code guys survive this
job. Damn! Every time I turned around, there was something
else I had to do! More pressure!

Along with these requirements for my job, Ski's position
as an HF/DF operative required an equally high level of performance, since both positions were considered by those in
charge of the station, and back in Washington, as the most
challenging and rewarding ones at NSG-Guam. At his position, Ski would be required to continuously monitor up to six
different frequencies on his receiver at the same time. As with
my position, he had to have high copying proficiency. Unlike
my position, however, his position at Guam was in the HF/DF
Section Headquarters, South Pacific Network, which required
a supervisory position, where the processing of all HF/DF
incoming and outgoing communications took place. This was
in anticipation of the installation of the planned AN/FRD-10
CDAA. The position would be manned by two or three senior

petty officers (CT-1s and CT-2s) as well as a chief petty officer (CPO) billet for that job. Ski wanted to qualify for certification for one of those jobs.

We learned that day that all of these responsibilities were just a small part of the overall SIGINT mission. As the "hunters and gatherers" position combined with the other branches of CTs changed, so would the NSA and NSG's mission, as its scope and magnitude constantly changed. No truer words were ever spoken.

Don't know how I accomplished it, but I made it through that first week of our orientation period and was gearing up for the next phase. By that I mean the first week I concentrated on monitoring and copying Soviet diplomatic traffic between Moscow and Pyongyang, North Korea. Mostly encrypted numeric blocks, each consisting of five numerals, strong signalization with few if any interruptions or frequency changes. Virtually all the transmissions couldn't have been better during most intercept sessions. On each of my watch shifts, I'd usually be occupied 75 or 80 percent of the time, and my copied volume was probably in the area of forty to forty-five intercepts per eight-hour watch, roughly fourteen thousand or more intercepts in a year.

Soviet diplomatic CW radio traffic between Moscow and Pyongyang was actually a pleasure, and I looked forward to my shifts. My copying speed was steadily increasing, my accuracy rate as well. I never really thought about it, but it was only two or so years after the Korean War, and the USSR was aggressively involved with their allies, the North Koreans. Everything was going just fine. And then, in the early spring of 1957, it all changed.

I was transferred to the ASW (anti-submarine warfare) section, where the best operatives were being assigned, as the Navy aggressively stepped up its development of defensive warfare in the face of increasing Soviet development of the nuclear-powered submarine as its primary offensive and defensive weapon. A nuclear-powered submarine is equipped with an SLBM (submarine-launched ballistic missile).

For hundreds of years, warring nations have sought to defend themselves during battle by setting up observation posts along key routes to their headquarters and strongholds. Early on, these actions consisted of as few as one observer, but oftentimes there were many observers, hiding in buildings or forested areas, keeping watch by sight. Soon, however, the warring nations developed networks of towers, communicating by such things as signal fires. Regardless of the means employed, the objective was the same: to gain advanced knowledge of the approach of one's enemy in order to enable defensive forces to be prepared in a timely manner. That strategy has developed step by step throughout history, but the technological means are radically different today. Now many, or perhaps most, of the tools for detection of enemy offensive and defensive weapons, as well as long-range observation techniques, are based on orbiting satellites. Instead of observing an enemy by sight, we use photographic reconnaissance by aircraft; and instead of signal fires for communications, we use radio signals that are relayed through satellites.

However, satellites today continue to have difficulties in the detection and tracking of submarines. Accordingly, since the late 1950s, one of the most challenging aspects of modern warfare has been the detecting and tracking of the deadliest weapon ever devised by man. It is this situation, first acknowledged in the Cuban Missile Crisis of 1962, that brought to the foreground the absolute need for detection and tracking of the submarine at any time and in any place.

One of the most successful ways of achieving this objective was the Sound Surveillance System (SOSUS), initially developed by the Navy in the early 1950s, prior to the launch of *Sputnik* by the USSR in October 1957. SOSUS was designed primarily as a result of the discovery of the propagation paths of sound through water. Early in its development, scientists had made a breakthrough discovery when they located a deepwater sound channel that trapped and compressed low-frequency sound waves, allowing them to travel over distances of thousands of miles. Up until this time, since World War I, sonar had been used with varying degrees of success to detect submarines over short distances, and by the end of World War II, radar was generally considered the premier sensor with which to locate submarines. But with SOSUS, a new fixed-location sonar system, an array of hydrophones deployed along the ocean floor in strategic areas of the Atlantic and Pacific, was deployed, which enabled the Navy to detect an enemy submarine as it left its home port or approached our waters. Bell Labs in 1950 had begun development of SOSUS as a vast network of seabed acoustic hydrophones that could utilize the characteristics of the deepwater sound channel. This system became a vital part of our defensive systems in the 1950s, during the time of a rapid buildup of the USSR's and other nations' submarine assets around the world.

SOSUS is a chain of U.S. Navy undersea listening posts located around the world in the Atlantic Ocean near Greenland, Iceland, and the U.K.—the so-called GIUK gap—and at numerous locations in the Pacific Ocean. The initial purpose for the system was for tracking Soviet submarines that had to pass through the gap or other locations—for example, to attack targets located west of the USSR.

The Navy's development of SOSUS began in 1949, when it was allocated $10 million to develop systems to counter the Soviet submarine threat, consisting at that time of a large fleet of diesel-powered submarines. The initial system was designed to monitor low-frequency sound in the deepwater sound channel, also called the SOFAR (sound-fixing and -ranging) channel, using multiple listening sites equipped with hydrophones and a land-based processing facility that could detect submarine positions by triangulation of radio communications over, at first, hundreds of miles but, later, up to 3,500 miles. A complement to the system was the Navy's AN/FRD-10 CDAA, developed shortly after the launch of *Sputnik* had led to a change in Soviet submarine communications systems to the "burst" system, which was patterned after the satellite's *"beep beep beep,"* a system originally developed by Germany during World War II.

The first hydrophone array was installed in 1950 on the island of Eleuthera in the Bahamas. By 1952, substantial progress resulted in plans to deploy six additional arrays in the North Atlantic, and the classified name of SOSUS was first used. The number of arrays was increased to nine by year's end, and in 1953 the project was expanded to include an additional high-frequency system for direct plotting of ships passing over the ocean-floor-based arrays, designed to be installed in narrows and straits.

By 1961, a year before the Cuban Missile Crisis, SOSUS had tracked the U.S. Navy's submarine USS *George Washington* (SSBN-598) from the East Coast of the U.S. to the United Kingdom. In mid-October 1962, during the Cuban Missile Crisis, the SOSUS system in the Bahamas tracked a Soviet Foxtrot-class submarine from the Mediterranean to Cuban waters. As submarines became quieter, generally due to nuclear-power operating systems, SOSUS was also upgraded to sustain its advantage in locating and tracking submarines, both diesel- and nuclear-powered.

Generally speaking, by the time of the Cuban Missile Crisis, a system of SOSUS land-based monitoring stations known as Naval Facilities Engineering Systems Command (NAVFAC) existed throughout the world, including Adak, Alaska; Whidbey Island, Washington; Pacific Beach, Washington; Coos Head, Oregon; Eel River, California; Monterey, California; San Nicolas Island, California; Barbers Point, Hawaii; Midway Island; Finegayan Beach, Guam; Yokosuka, Japan; Subic Bay, Philippines; Oceana, Virginia; Lewes, Delaware; Winter Harbor, Maine; Shelburne, Nova Scotia; Argentia, Newfoundland;

San Salvador, Bahamas; Bermuda; Grand Turk; Antigua; Barbados; Keflavik, Iceland; Brawdy, Wales, U.K.; Saint Mawgan, Cornwall, U.K.; Gibraltar; Rota, Spain; and Andøya, Norway.

Given its criticality to Cold War operations against the USSR's submarine fleet, SOSUS remained highly classified from its inception—and the purpose and activities of the various NAVFAC stations were not publicly acknowledged or commonly known outside of the Navy's submarine fleet and its ASW activities until the end of the Cold War. SOSUS had, however, played a key role in the resolution of the Cuban Missile Crisis in October 1962.

With the ending of the Cold War in 1991, the immediate need for SOSUS decreased substantially, and the focus of the Navy turned toward a system that was deployable on a war theater basis: the deployment of satellite-based defensive systems such as PARCAE ("White Cloud"). Ocean surveillance satellites continue to play a most important role in tracking ships and submarines around the globe, and their descendants will continue to orbit silently overhead well into the future, listening for the electromagnetic whispers and communications from ships at sea.

Whether it's a war between conventional adversaries or with terrorist cells such as ISIS, the great significance and importance of SIGINT and the intelligence community has never been greater than it is today.

SIX

SPUTNIK, WHALES, AND SOVIET SUBMARINES

The date was October 4, 1957, 2228 Moscow time, at Tyura-tam launch base in the Kazakh Soviet Socialist Republic. The former Soviet Union successfully launched *Sputnik 1,* the world's first artificial satellite. It was about the size of a basketball, weighed only 184 pounds, and took about 96 minutes to orbit the Earth. *Sputnik* traveled at 18,000 miles per hour in an elliptical orbit of from 584 miles (apogee) to 143 miles (perigee) above Earth.

That launch ushered in new political, military, technological, and scientific developments. While the *Sputnik* launch was a single event, it marked the start of the Space Age and the beginning of a fiercely competitive space race between the U.S. and the USSR.

Sputnik's radio transmission was in the form of "*beep beep beep*," about two *beep*s per second, which could be heard clearly anywhere in the world. This new radio format gave rise shortly after to the Soviet "burst" submarine Morse code radio transactions, which I had to search for in the Mariana Trench off Guam, among numerous Soviet submarines.

After World War II, the U.S. assumed that the USSR would rebuild their submarine fleet using what remained of the

German submarine fleet and its related communications systems, both offensively and defensively. Fortunately for the U.S., the Navy had developed and implemented an extensive Atlantic and Pacific submarine detection network, which they had improved over the World War II years and into the early 1950s. However, the Soviet launch of *Sputnik* in October 1957 and the subsequent development of the "burst" communications system for its submarine fleet dramatically increased the Navy's need for more extensive anti-submarine warfare (ASW) intelligence-gathering techniques and equipment. World War II had demonstrated without question how powerful "picture-based" detection could be.

HF/DF (high-frequency direction-finding) remained critical, and the World War II systems were rapidly updated, starting with shore-based "elephant cage" arrays and ship- or air-based short-range HF/DF antenna arrays installed on converted Navy ASW ships and aircraft. However, the Navy's future appeared grim in the mid-1950s, before these systems could be developed and placed in service. Accordingly, the Navy had to rely on land- and ocean-based ships for reports of merchant ship sinkings from submarine attacks.

A technological solution to the problem soon appeared, based on knowledge the Navy had discovered in the late 1940s, including the fact that low-frequency sound traveled great distances through the ocean. It was called SOSUS (Sound Surveillance System). Combined with other knowledge and research looking at the sound spectrum produced by a submarine, the Navy learned that submarines had distinct "signatures." That fact made it possible for SOSUS to locate a specific submarine at a specific place at a specific time. This information could be strung together to form continuous soundtracks that enabled SOSUS to accurately predict a submarine's physical position and course and immediately inform a ship or aircraft to intercept and attack the enemy boat.

Unfortunately, once the USSR developed the "burst" radio

transmission capability, its submarines might avoid detection simply because the radio transmission was of extremely short duration and virtually immune from interception. However, once a submarine was located, it was placed in a SOSUS submarine probability area (SPA), which was typically an extremely large surface or underwater area. The farther the submarine was from the antenna array, the larger the SPA. The search area, therefore, expanded as time elapsed. If a search aircraft were ASW-equipped, it could search the expanding SPA rapidly enough to have an excellent chance of finding the submarine. It also helped that the Navy's "JEZEBEL" sonobuoys used the same sound-analysis technique as SOSUS.

By the early 1960s, SOSUS and newly developed and activated HF/DF antenna arrays became the basis of a network-centered ASW system. These remote sensors fed data for evaluation into worldwide operations centers, which created a picture for ASW operations centers and for the Atlantic and Pacific fleet command centers. Much like with SOSUS, the development and implementation of the elephant cage array by the Navy was critical. With a range of up to 3,200 miles and utilizing "triangulation techniques," the Navy was able to locate and trace Soviet submarines virtually anywhere in the world, and it could plot them for continuous update activity.

Also of great significance, SOSUS was more effective against nuclear submarines than diesel ones because nuclear submarine noise-making propulsion machinery operates continuously; it can't turn off its nuclear reactor. For some unknown reason, throughout the 1960s, the USSR failed to silence its fleet of submarines. Only with the late, second-generation nuclear-powered submarines did they finally put in place a silencing program. However, even had there been no HF/DF advancement, SOSUS alone would have eventually rendered the Soviet submarine fleet, including its nuclear-powered submarines, obsolete as an offensive weapon delivery system.

In summary, initially SOSUS was primarily a way to locate submarines so that convoys could avoid them, but its "picture-based" display of Soviet underwater activity offered much more of an advantage in later years, especially during the Cuban Missile Crisis. As early as 1957, the "picture" was seen as a strategic warning indicator. As long as the USSR's submarines operated within SOSUS detection range (which was virtually everywhere), the picture generated was highly valued for its strategic defense capability.

With the Navy's elephant cage antenna arrays in place as well, the USSR had no offensive weapons—including effective guided missiles launched from nuclear-powered submarines deep under the surface of the world's oceans—with which to mount a long-range offensive attack against the U.S. As a result, before the Cuban Missile Crisis, the Navy had effectively developed and put in place a defensive surveillance system that enabled it to locate, track, and monitor any Soviet submarine anywhere in the world at any time. And the system had been activated.

As a Morse code operative with Naval Intelligence, assigned to ASW activities off Guam and in the Mariana Trench, I monitored Soviet submarines that were diesel-powered rather than nuclear-powered. To radio-intercept operatives, this meant that most CW radio traffic between Soviet submarines and their home port of Vladivostok was conducted after the submarine either had surfaced or had raised its antenna out of the water above sea level while remaining submerged. In other words, a surfaced or out-of-water antenna array can use ordinary radio communication; that is, they can transmit using Naval frequencies in the HF, VHF, and UHF frequency bands, using both voice and Morse code formats.

Looked at practically, HF/DF operations in the early days of World War II were by no means as simple as they were at the time *Sputnik* was launched. Still, at the time of *Sputnik*, there were few maps indicating local physical obstacles and magnetic deviations that negatively impacted the reliability and accuracy of radio waves—especially accuracy at long distances. It was necessary to learn by experience how deviations in a DF (direction-finding) wave behaved in the terrain between the transmitting station and the direction finder.

When a direction was fixed, it was critical to know whether the fixed station (the target) lay at a distance of 100, 200, 500 miles, or more. Enormous amounts of data had to be gathered and collated. At the time of the *Sputnik* launch by the USSR in October 1957, the Navy's capability was soon greatly expanded, from roughly 250 miles to approximately 2,500 miles in the late 1950s. This was principally because it became apparent to the Navy in the mid-1950s that the USSR's main offensive nuclear weapon was nuclear-powered submarines with the capability of launching SLBMs (submarine-launched ballistic missiles) from under the sea.

To the Navy, this meant that a Soviet ICBM (intercontinental ballistic missile), typically the R-7, with a payload ranging from 220 kilotons to 20 megatons, could be launched undetected, with a capability of reaching speeds of up to 20,000 miles per hour, with an effective range of 5,000 miles and altitudes of thousands of feet, within minutes after the launch.

This became apparent in 1957 with the launch of *Sputnik* and a corresponding change in Soviet submarine radio communications that rendered the old systems obsolete. Soviet submarines suddenly became silent and undetectable to U.S. intelligence. Accordingly, Naval HF/DF operations achieved their greatest importance in the Naval radio-intercept service. Coincidental with the *Sputnik* launch from Tyuratam Range in the Kazakh Soviet Socialist Republic was the fact that the USSR's nuclear-powered submarine and SLBM production soon moved from Vladivostok (Sea of Japan) and Murmansk (Barents Sea) to Odessa and Balaklava (Black Sea) in the late 1950s.

As you may recall, the communications from *Sputnik* as it circled around the Earth were in the format of a *"beep beep beep"*—each *beep* of extremely short duration—which made it very easy to track. The transmission itself had been electronically compressed so that a message was comprised of many groups of encoded alpha or numeric blocks, all transmitted in a matter of seconds, compared with minutes in the past. The new "burst" submarine transmission was nearly identical to the *Sputnik*'s "beep" transmission. The first such burst transmissions of the USSR were initially discovered among humpback whale calls by Navy signals intelligence operatives. Some of these transmissions came from the Mariana Trench off Guam, where I was listening from a Navy submarine.

The port of Vladivostok was the USSR's most important submarine base in its Pacific fleet, and as such, it was the principal target of the U.S. Navy's intelligence surveillance mission—specifically, the Navy's ASW program on Guam. Vladivostok is located on the northwestern coast of the Sea of Japan, while another Soviet submarine base was located at Petropavlovsk on the Kamchatka Peninsula, where in the 1960s a major fleet of nuclear submarines would be stationed. The major area for the construction and development of nuclear-powered submarines and SLBMs was in the Odessa-Balaklava area in the Black Sea.

Little did Ski and I know at the time, however, that our next duty station, in 1958, would be in North Africa, in the Mediterranean Sea area, with a focus on the nuclear submarines ported in the Black Sea at Odessa and Balaklava (Sevastopol) on the Crimean Peninsula. As it was in those times, both the U.S. and the USSR traditionally honored these territorial waters by operating within established international limits. On Guam, these limits included certain areas of the Mariana Trench, an area where the greatest oceanic depth on Earth, over 36,000 feet, is located, near the Challenger Deep, about two hundred miles southwest of Guam.

It wasn't until sometime in November 1957 that we found out that although the U.S. was operating with four or five submarines from Apra Harbor on Guam in the Trench, the USSR was simultaneously operating in the same area with between seven to ten submarines. Both the U.S. and the USSR were conducting SIGINT missions, principally involving non-nuclear submarines, with the USSR concentrating its surveillance missions on U.S. military activities at Andersen Air Force Base (a U.S. Air Force SAC base) and Naval Base Guam on Apra Harbor, headquarters of U.S. Naval Operations, South Pacific. Both the U.S. and the USSR greatly expanded their SIGINT activities in the area during the late 1950s, continuing through the 1960s and well into the 1990s, when the USSR was dissolved on December 26, 1991. These activities greatly expanded after the deployment by both countries of nuclear-powered submarines and SLBMs in the 1960s. The activities were a deadly game played with the highest stakes, as evidenced by the Cuban Missile Crisis in October 1962.

After monitoring and intercepting submarine radio communications for over a year on Guam, in October 1957 I found myself about to be assigned temporary duty aboard a submarine patrolling in the Mariana Trench as part of an ASW mission. The next thing we knew, four of us were told to report to the operations building the scheduled day of our EVE watch for a special briefing. We were to report to our watch section leader, who would give us more instructions. When we arrived the next afternoon around 1600, we were ushered into a conference room equipped with a movie projector, screen, tape drives, and two small tables on which a series of books and what appeared to be "reports" had been placed. Four stacks, one for each of us.

What's all this? A few minutes later a lieutenant came into the room with his assistant carrying a large box; he introduced himself and discharged his assistant. He placed the box in the center of our table, opened it, took out a magnetic tape and a roll of film, loaded one of the tape drives, and mounted the film on the movie projector. "What's all this about?" I muttered under my breath.

Before we could say anything, he turned on the tape drive. Lord! We were blasted, to say the least, by a tremendous outpouring of what sounded to us like electronic squeals, moans, and grunts up and down a whole range of frequencies. Turning down the sound, he explained that what we were hearing was the "singing" of the humpback whale, recorded recently in the Mariana Trench. He said further that every part of a whale's song is made up of sound waves, some of which are high-frequency and some low-frequency. He said that if we could "see" these waves, they would look like mountain peaks and valleys, the low-frequency sounds would be the valleys, spread wide apart, while the high-frequency sounds would look like the mountain peaks. These sound waves could travel very far in water without losing energy. With that statement, he nearly blew us away. He said that whale researchers had determined that some of the low-frequency sounds could, and did, travel more than five thousand miles at certain levels of the ocean depth. What? From there on Guam to Hawaii, nearly five thousand miles away? Impossible!

The first question we had was "So, what does this have to do with us?"

He turned up the sound, adjusted the pitch and other characteristics of the calls, and let it play for a minute or two. Then he cut off the recording, looked at us, and said, "What did you hear?"

None of us said anything. We were too stunned.

"Come on, sailors, get with it," he said. He turned on the tape again. "Listen," he said.

After a short span of maybe ten to fifteen seconds, one of the guys said, "I think I heard Morse code—real brief, though."

The lieutenant stopped the tape again. "Welcome to the real world, sailors. That was exactly what you heard. Morse code. But that's not what we want you to hear, so listen again."

We did, and once again, nothing.

Then he said, "First of all, what you heard at first was the humpback whale call, a male humpback whale call recorded deep in the Mariana Trench."

"You mean to tell us that mixed in among a humpback whale call was a Morse code radio transmission?" What was that all about?

We'd just experienced, not more than two or three days earlier, that the Soviet submarines we'd been tracking and monitoring in the Mariana Trench for months on end had suddenly "gone silent" on us. Except for sonar and radar contact, we wouldn't have known that they were even in the Trench anymore.

"Well," the lieutenant said, "they're still there, in the Trench, and the Navy is extremely worried about the situation. I mean extremely worried."

The lieutenant then told us that a former World War II Naval intelligence operative, now a chief petty officer stationed somewhere in Europe, had recently recalled something about a system of "burst" radio transmissions developed by the Germans toward the end of World War II and wondered if perhaps the USSR had perfected that system for their submarine fleet. Accordingly, NSA in Washington had begun to aggressively pursue this possibility and needed the assistance of the Naval Security Group to look into it. It was a fact that Bell Labs had been working on it for some time as well.

Now we knew what was going on there that day. The four of us had recently been selected for TDA aboard a submarine based at Apra Harbor there on Guam. We'd be on rotating duty of three days of near "around the clock" intercept duty, followed by three days off, then three days on again, for a two-week period, starting in a week or so. Any objections?

"Any objections?" What choice did we have after today's

meeting? It was a done deal. No turning back now. Besides, I'd often thought what it must be like to be aboard a submarine. I was damned sure going to find out now whether I liked it or not!

He then had us wait a moment while he filtered out the tape-recorded sounds and told us to listen closely. After he'd filtered out the CW Morse code transmission that one of us had said he thought he'd heard, the lieutenant said, "Now, plug in your headphones again and put them on." We did. "Here we go," he said.

Whoa! We all heard it: a "burst" electronic sound, duration of less than a second, then another, and it was over.

He turned the tape drive off. "Someone, describe what you heard," he said.

I don't recall who it was—I was too stunned to even think at that moment—but one of the guys, recalling his intelligence school training at Imperial Beach, raised his hand and said, "It sounds like that 'burst' radio transmission first developed by the Germans during World War II, or something like that."

The lieutenant said, "You're right, sailor. That's exactly what the Navy thinks it is." He then went on to tell us that toward the end of World War II, the Allies' success in DF, as in direction finding as the primary method to locate and track both German surface ships and U-boats had become a major and serious concern to the German high command. Their answer to the problem was to create a communications system that emphasized the use of extremely short radio signals, principally by U-boats, their most formidable weapon, that would enable them to communicate tactical information, such as course, enemy positions, weather, and other important information, at a rate of but a fraction of previous communications methods at the time, thereby virtually eliminating the Allies' ability to intercept their communications.

Their answer was *Kurzsignal,* or *Kurier,* developed by compressing Morse code radio signals electronically (known as "burst" encoding) designed as a countermeasure against DF.

The heart of the new system at the transmitting station centered upon attaching a synchronous electric motor to the device to precisely time the revolutions of the pulse generator. Each pulse was 1 millisecond long, and there was a 3-millisecond gap between each pulse. The pulse generator could be programmed to transmit a three-figure group (for entity identification) followed by a four-figure group (the *Kurier*) within 460 milliseconds. Therefore, the system became a serious threat to Allied Naval Intelligence, and no *Kurier* transmissions were ever successfully DF'd (i.e., found by high-frequency direction-finding [HF/DF] equipment).

The receiving station was equipped with three receivers, each with its own antenna and all tuned to the same U-boat frequency, using a complex broadcast schedule. The incoming signals were converted into pulses on a CRT (a cathode-ray tube, an "old-school, green-screen" computer terminal) and then photographed onto film; afterward, they were decoded upon development of the film.

This element of the entire *Kurier* system was still in the development stage when the war ended. The basic system, "burst radio," was captured by the USSR at war's end and fully developed in time for the *Sputnik* launch in October 1957, which employed a "*beep beep beep*" form of transmission rather than a "burst" format for its communications tasks. Had this not been the case, there is a strong possibility that the Navy's development of the AN/FRD-10 CDAA and programs such as SOSUS would not have existed at the time of the Cuban Missile Crisis in 1962.

We now knew that the situation of the "silent" submarines in the Mariana Trench was the implementation of the *Kurier* burst radio program for the USSR's submarine fleet.

So now I can give you a little background on this study of the humpback whales and what it had to do with the four of us in that room. Sometime after the launch of *Sputnik* and the loss of Soviet submarine radio transmissions, we learned that the Navy had undertaken a plan to "search for evidence"—electronic or other forms of communications—in the area the Navy was patrolling off Guam in the Mariana Trench. We subsequently learned that the search would be concentrated in certain areas that were known to support whales of various types. At that time, due to Guam's U.S. territorial status, the management of whales and other mammals in the Commonwealth of the Northern Mariana Islands was the jurisdiction of the U.S. National Marine Fisheries Service. It was this organization that assisted the Navy in determining what might be taking place in whale environments in the western Pacific to help us discern Soviet submarine radio transmissions. There had been few scientific surveys focused on large whale distribution, but it was known that a relatively large number of humpback whales were in our area at that time of the year.

In layman's terms, the National Marine Fisheries Service suggested that the Navy might want to tape-record and analyze the humpback's "vocalizations" for some clues. And that is how certain of us were selected for TDA aboard a submarine in the Trench. SIGINT would equip space on the submarine for us to undertake around-the-clock monitoring via tape-recording of humpback whale calls. Our survey coverage area would be over a wide range of depths, and it would be subject to certain weather and sea conditions, together with certain speed restrictions. The plan was presently being developed back in Washington, D.C., after which we would begin our mission. In the meantime, those of us on TDA would be listening at our base to already-recorded humpback whale calls as well as just what the Navy already thought we might be able to uncover: an electronically produced "burst" radio transmission of not more than a second in duration, followed by another. And another. And we had Sputnik to thank for this crucial discovery!

Our tour of duty on Guam was over in November 1958. I would have a thirty-day leave. I cleaned out my locker; took down all the pictures I'd gathered over the past eighteen months—probably about thirty or so—sold or gave away my swim mask, snorkel, flippers, fishing rod, Hawaiian sling speargun, golf putter, tennis racket, mugs and glasses from local bars, and shell collection; and threw out old civilian shirts, pants, and other unnecessary clothes.

Warm early morning breeze off the water. Beautiful day. Bon voyage, Apra Harbor, Guam. Berth of the USS *Virgo*, AKA-20, a World War II attack cargo ship—destination: Port Chicago, near San Francisco, California.

Thank God they got the gangplank right. Otherwise, there's no way any of us could ever have made it up carrying seabags and other stuff. Either my seabag or I would have been in the water! Probably both!

Got my seabag on my shoulder, my other hand partially on the line and partially on my handbag, up the plank, steadily, but slowly, till I'm there. Salute the colors; salute the OOD (officer of the deck): "Permission to come aboard, sir!" He nods. Finally, a solid foot on deck, make my way over to the MAA (master-at-arms), hand him my orders, and he directs me to the transient quarters, forward, up beneath the bow. Beneath the bow? Looks like automatic seasickness to me. We'll see.

A few minutes later, after locating my bunk in the forward berthing quarters under the bow, I change from dress whites to my dungarees, as directed, and report topside to assist with the getting-underway mooring detail. In other words, standing around for the next hour or so while they continue loading the hull compartments from the dock. Finally, we are ready to depart. Tug on the starboard bow, detail pulling lines, circling on deck, tugboat horns, we're away.

Yeah, this was the USS *Virgo*, the same ship detailed in the 1955 movie *Mr. Roberts* (although there was no palm tree on the bridge) from the book written by Thomas Heggen (who served on the *Virgo*), with Henry Fonda as Mr. Roberts and Jack Lemmon as Ensign Pulver. I was long out of the Navy before I realized I'd been on *that Virgo*.

The USS *Virgo* was on the final leg of her journey from Guam to Hawaii and on to the Mare Island Naval Shipyard, Vallejo, California, for decommissioning in April 1958. She was a grand old ship, launched in 1943; she earned seven battle stars in World War II, nine in Korea, and ten in Vietnam. She was sold for scrap in November 1973. A fine, thirty-year career.

Soon the tugboat maneuvered alongside, a port pilot boarded the *Virgo* and guided her out of the harbor into the open Pacific. The pilot descended from the *Virgo* by rope ladder to the deck of the tug, and we were underway, on our twenty-one-day voyage home, with a brief layover in Hawaii, where the rumor was that we would be moored nearby the site of the USS *Arizona*.

While we were not considered "crew members," we would be assisting the numerous crews aboard the ship during the entire journey, and we would be observing in other areas of the ship's various departments, such as Operations, Radar, Radio, Combat Information Center, ASW, Bridge, Signal (whose personnel were practicing flag-hoisting drills and flashing-light drills), and Engineering (where the ship's crew underwent continuous instruction and practice in the operation of the ship's engines, including how to operate the ship in the case of loss of power, especially in inclement weather). Even the MAA was involved, carrying out .45-caliber pistol instruction on the fantail. And we would spend lots of time in the commissary and the mess area, hearing instructions in the proper storage of perishable food supplies, as well as lectures on food sanitation and the storage of cooking utensils and the like. These were the guys who would provide the ship's crew and transients with three meals a day. Quite a job for a ship with a crew complement of some sixty men. It's a totally new experience for the four of us from the Naval Intelligence base, who hadn't done this type of work since we were in boot camp. The shift crew had a great time "educating" us in their line of work.

That first afternoon, around 1500, General Quarters sounded, and the entire ship's crew, excluding those of us in transit, dressed in battle dress and proceeded to their assigned stations. Since we were to remain in our quarters, we didn't get to see any of that "drill." One unusual drill we did get to observe was the "Man Overboard" drill. It took two men, plus the officer on the ship's bridge, to slow the ship down and bring it around to pick up the "overboard dummy." Two sailors, with grappling hooks and lines, retrieved the dummy. Hard job. First try, the sailor missed the dummy, and the other sailor had to run back to the fantail area and try to retrieve the dummy—which he did successfully. Got a good "Navy cheer" from the observing sailors, as well. As a result, the ship had to complete the "rescue" only once, not the usual twice around again and try once more. Boring task but one that's necessary—especially if you happened to be the sailor who fell overboard!

It was nearly 1630 now; the crew work for the day was done, and chow call was sounded. Great meal, nearly as good as ours back on the intelligence base. After chow, movies were shown in the wardroom and the crew's mess compartment for all those hands not on an assigned watch. "Taps" was sounded at 2200, and most of the crew and transients were ready to hit the rack. Another new experience: In the bow transit quarters, there was considerably more "motion" than in most other areas of the ship. And I mean plenty of motion from the sea. Those transients who weren't used to the motion nearly always got seasick. Especially guys who had never been to sea before. It was gonna be one hell of a long trip, believe me—especially for Ski. He had already been seasick just from the initial departure from the docks at Apra Harbor into the Pacific, but after about five minutes here in the bow, he was gone. *He was sick!* What made it all the worse was that he was pissed off at me simply because I didn't get seasick. Not even once on the entire twenty-one-day trip.

Man, was I glad I'd had that experience on the *High Hopes* back in high school! And that my dad had initiated me well when I was just a little guy out on the Connecticut River fishing for shad and in the Atlantic fishing for blues. You just never know when some of your childhood experiences are going to come in handy, but I sure was grateful after about an hour in that compartment under the bow of the ship. We had two heads, but we needed at least ten more! Tough break, sailor. Welcome to the real Navy!

Little did we know at that moment just what was in store for us about ten days ahead. We hadn't seen or experienced anything yet, but at that moment, a late-season hurricane (in the Pacific they're called "typhoons") named "Nina," a category 1 storm, with sustained winds of roughly eighty miles per hour, was south of Hawaii and was heading north toward the Hawaiian Islands but was expected to track westerly in a few days. It was coming to visit *Virgo,* and we'd never forget it. It was of considerable concern to the captain and crew of the *Virgo,* and they were watching the storm's progress closely. They got really concerned when they learned that the storm had changed direction and was now moving toward the west, in our direction.

In my younger days in Fort Lauderdale, I had been through two or three hurricanes and was well aware of the damage they were capable of inflicting. Ski and some of the other guys in our quarters asked me about hurricanes, and I spent a good bit of time describing them. I soon realized I'd made a grave mistake—they were now all frightened to death—and so was I, just remembering the intensity of the winds and the power of the water. In 1947, before a hurricane hit Fort Lauderdale at our beach home, we had been caught in high surf that was, by the time we left the house for shelter at my grandfather's Packard dealership, nearly up to the road (A1A) out of our neighborhood from where the surf normally broke on the beach, about forty to fifty yards from the road. In fact, several waves broke against our car as we got underway, and we were lucky to make it to the main road west from the beach into Fort Lauderdale proper.

I knew that things here on the *Virgo* were not good, and they were deteriorating rapidly. There was absolutely nothing we could do about it. We were experiencing much stronger seas; our speed had slowed to around twelve to fifteen knots. We were heading east, the storm was heading west, and there was no shelter for us. Pearl Harbor was roughly seven hundred to eight hundred miles away, and we were in the middle of the Pacific Ocean. I didn't like it, period. But there was nothing at all that anyone could do to change the situation. Nothing at all.

I was on the bridge, along with six to eight other officers and enlisted men. The previous night the captain had asked if there were any "transit" personnel on board who did not suffer from seasickness. If so, they were to report to the bridge. Of the eighteen of us, only one other guy besides me had reported and given the captain our backgrounds. I told him I wasn't a true sailor in the sense that I'd been to sea on a Naval ship before, but I had considerable experience as a mate on a charter boat back home in Fort Lauderdale, knew the seas from the Gulf Stream, and had, in fact, fallen overboard on a particularly rough day. I was told to "stand by" in our quarters until contacted.

I sensed that Ski was somewhat concerned, since he had been sick on and off most of the last day or so. I was told that extra crew were sometimes requested to be available in the event that seasickness got out of hand. Fortunately, it never affected me, and I was able to assist with certain readings and situations as the day progressed. It was a truly incredible experience, to be frank. There was extreme pressure on those of us on the bridge and in the engine room below, and as it all subsided late that afternoon, I had a profound respect for the captain of the *Virgo*. Even now, I don't like to think about what could have been the outcome that day.

The *Virgo* had been rolling maybe fifteen to twenty degrees since late the night before, and the sea had picked up substantially when a member of the crew entered our quarters in the morning and asked for me. He, another crewman, and I then proceeded to work our way to the bridge between those rolls, which to me was not a pleasant experience. Probably because I knew it was going to get one hell of a lot worse. And soon. No problems for the next few hours, with the exception of the fact that the seas continued to worsen, almost steadily.

I was assigned to assist two deck personnel call out readings on a critical piece of equipment: the clinometer. One of the most important instruments on a ship during inclement weather is the clinometer. It's a device that measures the angles of the Earth's surface, and in the marine industry, they're used to measure how much a ship "slants" while being on still water and when the water is really bad, as in a hurricane. Well, to me, it was the most important instrument on the ship because I knew that if you rolled too much, you were gone. Period. That one piece of equipment was critical because it indicates to the captain whether the angle of the ship's rolling is at or near the danger line. (We had a similar instrument on the *High Hopes*.) That was something I really wanted to know. Now. Immediately.

My stress level was skyrocketing. Had to get it under control. Finally got a chance to see the instrument, but I couldn't really see anything, because the two sailors tending it blocked my view, but I could hear them report, with increasing frequency a starboard roll to thirty-five degrees, followed by a port roll of forty degrees or so, somewhere in this area. I can't remember the actuals. I do, however, seem to recall that you would really start to worry if the angle approached sixty-five or so degrees. The situation took me back to high school days, when I'd more than once experienced rolls of forty to forty-five degrees on the *High Hopes* while fishing in the Gulf Stream.

Soon I was noticing that the port wing of the bridge, then the starboard wing, was dipping under and scooping up the blue-green water as the ship continued to yaw and roll heavily. You'd hear the engines rev as the captain increased the ship's speed in an effort to ease the steering, but this in turn meant long, surfing-like runs down the swells with huge rollers at the end, when the ship was brought to a pause in the rough of the wave. The cycle would then start over again when the next swell picked up the ship and pushed it forward. In the valley between the swells, the ship would roll heavily, port to starboard, starboard to port, while the sailors on the bridge would look up, not out, at the seas. This went on for approximately six to eight hours. It was an event that is extremely hard to describe, almost impossible to bear, and it impacted each and every sailor on the *Virgo*—probably me the most! I was freaked out, to say the least.

As the winds increased, the seas also became larger. But in spite of increasing heavy weather, the captain had steering control from the bridge, as far as I can remember, and we were experiencing deep rolls of thirty-four to forty-five degrees during much of the time, whenever I had a chance to glance at the clinometer. I learned something else after it was all over. The design of the ship's bridge somehow lowered the center of wind pressure on the hull, which in turn had reduced the level of roll of the ship in the storm while the bridge structure itself appeared to be under heavy stress at times from the wind. The worry, if any, was that the bridge itself could possibly be torn from the ship. During most of the afternoon, the average strength of the wind reported by the equipment ranged from roughly forty-five to sixty knots, with gusts as high as seventy to seventy-five knots, just over hurricane strength. I don't recall what the low barometric pressure was, but it was probably likely in the low to mid 28.0 inches. Much lower, and you're in real trouble.

Eventually, the seas were subsiding, the speed of the winds and gusts falling, and the roll was down to a controllable twenty to twenty-five degrees. We had made it. Survived. There could not have been a sailor on that ship who felt any better than I did at that time. It had been bad at times on the *High Hopes*, but I was just a kid—what did I know back then? This was the Navy, two thousand miles at sea. As I write this, I have discovered that a Navy rollover event is not uncommon. During a December 1944 hurricane, as ships of the U.S. Third Fleet were attempting to fuel east of the Philippines, they were overtaken by a strong hurricane, which resulted in the capsizing and sinking of three destroyers, the USS *Hull*, the USS *Monaghan*, and the USS *Spence*. Search results conducted by other ships and aircraft resulted in the rescue of just a few officers and men: seven officers and fifty-five sailors from the *Hull*, six sailors from the *Monaghan*, and one officer and twenty-three sailors from the *Spence*. Approximately eight hundred men were lost at sea. Events such as this continue to happen to this day.

The officers and sailors of the USS *Virgo* were fortunate, and by late afternoon that day, we were well on our way to Pearl Harbor. The sea journey of roughly 4,750 miles to San Francisco would soon be over. Dismissed by the captain, I was on my way back to our quarters in the bow of the ship. Once I got to the bow, I moved to the hatchway, opened the hatch, eyed the berth area as the smell rose to greet me. I hesitated, grabbed my nose, and moved down the ladder.

I've got to get Ski up and out of here, I thought. Jesus!

Except for the ship's crew, I was probably the only one who could stand up and move about, and who had a clean uniform. God, the stench! Diarrhea and vomit at the same time, and what was so bad was the fact that virtually all the guys were in the same shape. Diarrhea and vomit, in and on their uniforms, on their fart sacks and pillows, on the deck, and in the head. Christ, it'll take a week just to clean it up! And the stench, good God—the stench was unbelievable. Some of the guys wouldn't have another uniform to put on, let alone new bedding. It was going to be one hell of a mess washing all the uniforms and bedding. Thank God the ship had plenty of hot water. A real blessing. When I got to Ski's bunk he was lying there in a mess of vomit and, I guessed, shit in his pants from the diarrhea that had started two days earlier, before the typhoon. Who knew what caused it? It hadn't affected me, and we ate the same meals. But it was the stench that really got to you. Ski looked up at me. Sorriest spectacle I'd ever seen—helpless and completely defeated, physically and mentally. But he managed a brief embarrassed-like smile and said one thing to me: "Bob, get me out of here!"

All I could think about at that moment was *Is this what it's like to be on a ship during wartime or, worse yet, in a foxhole on the battlefield?* There was nothing funny about any of this, just two close buddies facing a serious situation and helping each other. Maybe that's what war—and this certainly wasn't war, by any means—ultimately comes down to: love and respect for your cubicle or foxhole mate during grave times. Going through a typhoon on a ship was one of those times. Not as dangerous as war, but bad just the same. I grabbed a towel from the bunk next to Ski; rummaged through his seabag until I found a pair of whites, the last pair of clean skivvies, a T-shirt, and a pair of socks; grabbed his last pillowcase and stuffed all of it inside; took him by the arm and up from his bunk; and grabbed his shoes on the way. God, did he stink! I pulled him by the arm as we moved as quickly as we could up the passageway and onto the deck. The ship was still cutting through the rough seas with lots of motion, so we were temporarily restricted to the immediate area of the forward compartment on the bow of the ship. There was a hose on the deck, which some of the more fortunate guys had used to hose off. I grabbed it, told Ski to take off his soiled skivvies and T-shirt, and hosed him down from the top of his head to his feet for about three to four minutes. I then took the towel and dried his head, hair, and back, best I could. He finished the job, put his skivvies on, and just sat there.

Finally, the first words out of his mouth were "Thanks, Bob."

I just looked at him and said, "You'd have done the same for me, brother. And let me tell you one more thing, brother: If you'll keep your eyes on the horizon—straight ahead, nowhere else—you'll soon feel a hell of a lot better."

He looked at me again and said, "How in the hell do you know that?"

I replied, "I just know it, believe me."

In retrospect, I know that after nearly two years together, I felt a real kinship to Ski. He was my "brother." We'd worked together on the job, played sports for ourselves and for our base, been in numerous fights on the base and on liberty, and were proud as hell of our profession. After about an hour, he regained his composure, got up, put on his last set of whites, and said, "Let's go to chow." He was back!

0600, December 9, 1957: While the regular crew of the *Virgo* had been at Pearl Harbor several times before, all of us transients were up early to watch the *Virgo* enter Pearl Harbor—especially to get the best viewing location on the bow and port side of the ship, anxious to see what it must have been like to have been in this same position on

December 7, 1941, the day the Japanese launched a surprise attack against the United States. Ski and I both remarked that we wished we had arrived two days earlier, on the sixteenth anniversary of the attack, and had the opportunity to participate in the ceremony. The sight was staggering, to say the least. There was still evidence everywhere of the near destruction of the port: remains of sunken or severely damaged ships, destroyed administration and storage buildings. Yet there was evidence of new and ongoing construction, rebuilt dockage, mooring, and refueling facilities, together with tremendous piles of damaged and abandoned scrap metal, buildings, and various unusable equipment and materials of all sorts waiting to be loaded, hauled away, and forgotten. It was a mind-boggling sight, one I vividly remember to this day.

What must it have been like for the thousands of servicemen who experienced that fateful day? Do we still remember? I thought about the significant strategic importance of signals intelligence in the avoidance of such catastrophic events. Through the years we've been told there was no such intelligence that could have possibly prevented this event. Is that true? Why? The Japanese certainly had all the intelligence they needed to conduct this attack. The Japanese had assembled a strike force consisting of 4 heavy aircraft carriers that launched over 350 aircraft, including 40 torpedo planes, 103 level bombers, 131 dive-bombers, and 79 Zero fighter planes. The attack fleet also consisted of 2 heavy cruisers, 2 light cruisers, 2 battleships, 11 destroyers, 9 refueling ships, and 35 submarines. The fleet had sailed from Japan several days before, to within roughly two hundred miles northwest of the Hawaiian Islands. And the U.S. had no evidence of their presence? What? Knowing what Ski and I knew, that didn't seem possible to us. But as a result of that fact, here is what we do know about the casualties resulting from the attack, which lasted just over an hour and fifteen minutes:

PEARL HARBOR ATTACK

U.S. Military Casualties			Japanese Military Casualties		
KILLED	WOUNDED	TOTAL	KILLED	WOUNDED	TOTAL
2,335	1,135	3,478	129	1	130

U.S. Ships			Japanese Ships		
DESTROYED	DAMAGED	TOTAL	DESTROYED	DAMAGED	TOTAL
3	16	19	5	0	5

U.S. Aircraft			Japanes Aircraft		
DESTROYED	DAMAGED	TOTAL	DESTROYED	DAMAGED	TOTAL
169	159	328	29	0	29

Frightening. But there is more to the story.

It was a calm, clear, beautiful day that fateful morning sixteen years earlier. Yet, two hundred miles away, the Japanese Navy was preparing to launch a near Armageddon-like strike against the United States, unknown to anyone on the undisturbed and beautiful islands, mountains, and beaches of Hawaii. On another island's mountaintop, a lone radio-intercept operative had reported for duty that Sunday morning around 0600. As he searched his assigned frequency band, heavy with voice and Morse code transmissions, he heard, faintly, a Japanese voice transmission that appeared to be repeating itself over and over. Only slightly familiar with the Japanese language, which he didn't speak or write, he paused, then asked the young Japanese cleaning boy who was working in the yard outside the radio shack to listen to the transmission. The boy was fascinated to be asked to listen to the earphones and eagerly put them on. He said, in broken English, "It sounds like 'East Wind, Rain,' and it repeats over and over." The intercept operator took the earphones from the boy and contacted his supervisor in Honolulu to report the unusual transmission. His contact in Honolulu paid no attention to the message, informing the operative that it was probably nothing to be concerned about. Even today, as you read this book, no one then or now seems to know what happened to that original message. In 1977 N. Richard Nash wrote a book entitled *East Wind, Rain,* which contains certain information about the message, obtained from the pilot of a Japanese Zero that crashed on a remote Hawaiian island not far from Pearl Harbor at the time of, or shortly before, the attack.

During World War II, Japan allegedly prearranged coded weather forecasts to alert its diplomats overseas of ensuing attacks on a foreign country. "North wind, cloudy" would mean the Soviet Union; "West wind, clear" meant Britain; "East wind, rain" meant the United States, or more specifically, Pearl Harbor on December 7, 1941.

Although some historians argue that Japan's "wind code" never was the intelligence indicator that it first appeared, Chinese actor-director Yunlong Liu used this World War II story as background for his directorial debut film, *East Wind Rain,* which is set in Shanghai before and after the attack on Pearl Harbor. (Source: cctv.com's News/Culture section, dated 2010-03-22 12:04 BJT.)

SEVEN

NORTH AFRICA

We left Anacostia Naval Station in Washington, D.C., for Charleston Air Force Base in South Carolina on February 12, 1958, for a MATS flight to Casablanca, Morocco, and the beginning of an eighteen-month tour of duty at Sidi Yahia el Gharb Naval Communications Station. After a stopover in the Azores, we finally arrived at Nouasseur Air Base around 0900 local time. Nouasseur Air Base was a U.S. Air Force base siting in the former French Morocco, developed out of the Allied presence there at the close of World War II. In the early 1950s, SAC (Strategic Air Command) developed an "Operation Reflex" strategy between its southern bases and Morocco, with B-36 and B-47 wings rotating to North Africa for extended temporary duty as a staging area for bombers pointed at the Soviet Union.

Casablanca is the largest city in Morocco, located in the west-central part of the country, bordering the Atlantic Ocean.[7] It is one of the largest and most important cities in Africa, both economically and demographically. It is Morocco's

---

7. The source for this paragraph and the next one is https://en.wikipedia.org/wiki/Casablanca.

chief port and one of the largest financial centers on the continent. The 2016 census (adjusted with recent numbers) recorded a population of about 6 million in the prefecture of Casablanca. Casablanca is considered the economic and business center of Morocco, although the national political capital is Rabat.

The leading Moroccan companies and international corporations doing Moroccan business have their headquarters and main industrial facilities in Casablanca. Recent industrial statistics show Casablanca retains its historical position as the main industrial zone of the country. The port of Casablanca is one of the largest artificial ports in the world; it is the second-largest port of North Africa. Casablanca also hosts the primary naval base for the Royal Moroccan Navy.

Casablanca was an important strategic port during World War II, and it hosted the Casablanca Conference in 1943, in which Churchill and Roosevelt discussed the progress of the war. Casablanca had been the site of a large American air base that was the staging area for all American aircraft for the European Theater of Operations during the war.

Although it was February when we arrived, it was relatively warm in Casablanca, with its location on the coast. Landing in Morocco was the last good thing that happened to us that fateful day! The moment the doorway of the plane opened and we saw a Navy jeep waiting for us, we knew we were someplace very, very different. From the air, Casablanca had looked to us like a mid-fifteenth-century city. Virtually every building—what we guessed were homes, shops, the *medina* (shopping areas with two- or three-story buildings), and virtually everything else—was white. No color, just white. Few trees or landscaping, with the exception of some type of palms. There was only one building over four stories high! And all of it was surrounded by what appeared to be a six-to-eight-foot-high white wall, of concrete or something related.

As far as we could see, around the entire city that was all; outside the wall there were no trees or vegetation, houses, or other buildings.

The streets in the city looked like nothing we had ever seen: literally hundreds of all types of vehicles—from bikes to wagons drawn by donkeys and camels, but with very few automobiles or trucks. When you could make out a car or truck, it appeared to be at least twenty to thirty years old, dating from the 1930s and 1940s, mostly pre–World War II years. Virtually all the people we could see were wearing white—shirts, robes, headwear, all of it white. Rather than much traffic noise, there were unusual sounds: animal cries, bellows, bells, shouts from their masters and drivers, coupled with the usual sound of horns from automobiles and trucks, which comprised maybe 10 to 11 percent of all the "traffic" we could see. Yet, at the time, it was a city of approximately 700,000 people of all types, nationalities, and races—mostly veiled and who knows what else. And an unusual smell was everywhere. I mean everywhere. A mixture of something. But not really too bad. But not good either.

The jeep soon made it through all the traffic commotion and outside the walls of the city, to a road that led to the coast, only a mile or so from the city. Soon we were on our way to Port Lyautey (now called Kenitra), north of Casablanca, also on the Atlantic coast, home of the U.S. Naval air station, where we would catch another ride to Sidi Yahia el Gharb, roughly fifteen miles east, toward the foothills of the Middle Atlas Mountains. I mean it was one hell of a relief to get out of all that commotion. Then we noticed the camels and their drivers and riders along the side of the road. And it was almost at that very moment that it hit us: the stench of camel excreta— feces and urine, all at the same time! And it was absolutely overpowering. I mean *overpowering*! Our driver immediately said, "You'll get over it. I can barely smell it anymore."

Truthfully, our driver didn't seem to be the least bit bothered about it at all. Ski asked him how long he'd been there, and he said, "Little over a year. Got six months to go."

God, it was awful. Something we never really got used to all the time we were in Africa, including on the camel tracks in the Sahara Desert in the ungodly heat. What really made it even worse was that every time our driver honked to pass a camel on the road, it would drop another load—as if to say, "Have another. Hope you enjoy it"—which we promptly ran over, throwing half of it under the wheel well and side of the jeep, to ride along with us. In all my life, I'd never experienced anything like it. And both of us said we could never, never adapt to the stench. It was virtually all the way to Port Lyautey, which—thank God—we finally reached after our journey into hell!

We weren't through with our journey from Casablanca to Sidi Yahia, however. As we got a Navy bus—and new driver—for the remainder of the trip, which was for a short while along the Sebou River, our driver said, "You guys see that body floating in the river? . . . Look near the shoreline. . . . It's floating out to the Atlantic. . . ." Then he said, "Happens all the time along the river. It's one of the ways the Mo's (Moroccans) get rid of the dead."

Ski and I looked at each other and said, "Jesus Christ!" both about the same time.

Our driver then said something like "They'll tell you more about it when we get to Sidi Yahia."

Ski and I looked at each other again and said something resembling "Holy shit, how in the name of hell did we get this GD duty station, anyway?"

I don't know what Ski thought, but I thought to myself, *If I could contact the guy who cut my orders to this GD place, I'd beat the shit out of the son of a bitch.*

True enough, later in the day, at orientation on the base, we were told, among other odd things, that if we were driving a vehicle on a roadway and hit a Moroccan citizen, we'd better be sure he was dead, because if not, the Moroccan government would order you to pay all his medical expenses and care for him the rest of his life. Even today I don't know if that was true or not, but anytime we left the base in a private vehicle, which thankfully was not too frequently, we'd spend half the time watching out for Mo's walking along the road. Fortunately, over there at that time, very few people actually walked along the roadways or drove vehicles. But they might be riding a camel.

Ski and I still couldn't get over the fact that we were there in North Africa for the next eighteen months. Eighteen months? *Holy shit, what is going on here?* From paradise on earth—Guam—in the Pacific Islands, with its unbelievable beaches, etc., to the gates of hell over here in North Africa in one simple transfer. *GD! Why us?* Then it dawned on me— *bam!* right between the eyes! Both Ski and I—since we'd first walked on the base at Sidi Yahia—had been wondering why we didn't see any seaman-rated CTs—i.e., three-stripers—on the base. All we had seen were petty officers like ourselves, from PO3s to CPOs and officers or Marines. Why was that? Then it dawned on us. This place was indeed a hell on earth, a real shock to the senses. Naval Intelligence wouldn't dare take the risk of sending someone just out of intelligence school, at age seventeen or so, to a place like this. You got sent to places like this only if you were "seasoned," an old salt who could handle about anything, especially a place like this. Yeah, that's what it was, we convinced ourselves. We were *men*! Believe me, you had to be to handle all this shit.

Still, we thought the Navy had to find a way to brace guys like us, who had previously been in paradise. There was nothing, absolutely nothing, like it. It had so far been pure living hell and it GD better get better, and soon. And it did, about ten minutes later.

We had finished our initial orientation and were directed

over to our assigned barracks. After opening the door, we started walking down a narrow passageway to our cubicle, which was the second from last. Ski, especially, was still really pissed off, to say the least, and it made it all the harder trying to navigate down a passageway lugging a full seabag and carry-on luggage. Some poor CT was simply standing by his locker, halfway blocking us. I say "poor" because what happened next took us back to Guam, the barracks, bus rides, bars and nightclubs—all of it. Ski's seabag bumped him slightly, and he muttered something that Ski didn't like. Ski turned to me, sweating—as was I because of the lack of air conditioning—his cuffs rolled up and hat falling down into his eyes, and said to me, like he had many, many times on Guam, "Bob, take him out, will ya?"

So, as I had many times before on Guam, I hit him with a left hook and watched him fall.

And once again, Ski said, "Nice shot"—except this time he added, "This place pisses me off." At least, that's what I thought he said, because he usually did. And I wasn't really paying that much attention to what he said.

I do recall thinking to myself, *Well, it had taken us less than two minutes or so to get into our first fight.* "Going to be a hell of a long eighteen months," I said to Ski.

He didn't reply. Both of us were tired and sweating from carrying our seabags and stuff and were just plain pissed off. So, what was one more fight?

We got to our cubicle, threw down our seabags, took the two bunks on the right—just like on Guam, me on the top rack, Ski on the bottom rack—put down our mattress covers (fart sacks) and pillows, which were in the bottom of our seabags, and went to sleep. When we woke up several hours later, it was dark, and we were hungry. Finally found a guy in the barracks, and he instructed us on the location of the gedunk, where we could get a sandwich and a beer, since the chow hall was closed. When we awoke again, around 2330 or so, we met our cube mates, a guy named Tierney and another named Tufto. That's all we knew, as they left for the MID watch.

Little did we know at that moment what lay ahead of us for those next eighteen months. In addition to Soviet submarines in the Black Sea and Soviet diplomatic radio traffic, the French-Algerian war would change our lives forever.

During our briefing in Washington, D.C., before leaving for North Africa, both Ski and I learned that we'd be assigned to the ASW unit, continuing the classified work we'd done on Guam. Both of us were pleased about that, knowing that we'd continue our Navy tour as "brothers" while in Africa. Initially, Africa seemed a strange place for the work we'd be doing, but other than that, we were looking forward to it as our next duty station.

We'd learned early after our assignment to ASW on Guam that one of the most challenging parts of ASW was clearly the detection, tracking, and interception of Soviet submarine communications, both on and below the surface. And in the Navy at this time in history, the most successful means of achieving this objective was the SOund SUrveillance System (SOSUS), developed by the Navy during the early 1950s. It was centered on discoveries at that time of the propagation paths of sound waves through water. Its intention, from the beginning, was to provide a means of locating, tracking, and monitoring the growing threat of Soviet submarines, with primary emphasis on nuclear-powered and -equipped submarines.

SOSUS initially provided a reliable method of locating and tracking Soviet submarines; it allowed for optimal positioning of ASW land and sea bases (such as the base on Guam and aboard specially outfitted ships, such as the USS *Liberty*, AGTR-5). SOSUS quickly took on a greater role with the advent of Soviet submarine-launched ballistic missile (SLBM) boats. SOSUS was the primary deterrent to the escalation of the Cuban Missile Crisis. Since the end of the Cold War in 1991, SOSUS has undergone a number of changes in its utilization, but until recently it was the primary military asset against the growing number of nuclear-powered and -equipped submarines around the world.

The central feature of SOSUS is a configuration of fixed sonar systems in an array of hydrophones deployed along the ocean floor in strategic areas, designed to detect an enemy submarine as it either leaves its home waters or approaches ours. The system was, and still is, extremely effective. The first such hydrophones could detect submarines from several miles away. Today (and during the Cuban Missile Crisis), the system can detect submarines from a distance of thousands of miles. This capability came about as a result of breakthrough discoveries during and after World War II. Scientists discovered the location of a deepwater sound channel that trapped and focused low-frequency sound waves, allowing them to propagate over such great distances. Bell Labs was the first to develop the concept of SOSUS, which was soon to become a vast network of seabed acoustic hydrophones that could utilize the characteristics of these sound channels to detect the presence of submerged submarines at long ranges.

Soon the Navy was preparing for implementation of the SOSUS network, and the first project, named JEZEBEL, was to be installed in the Bahamas in the early 1950s by Bell Labs. It was so successful that in 1952, the Navy began to install SOSUS arrays along the entire eastern coastline of the U.S. Two years later, plans were developed to install SOSUS arrays along the western coastline and in the ocean waters surrounding Hawaii. Both these systems were completed and began operations in 1958, around the time Ski and I arrived in Africa.

The way that SOSUS worked was basically this: The detection network of arrays was connected to land-based Naval facilities that would receive and process the acoustic information. This refined data would then be passed on to "evaluation centers" (such as our base on Guam and here in Africa), which would incorporate other sources, such as high-frequency direction-finding (HF/DF) equipment and certain antenna arrays such as the AN/FRD-10 CDAA system on Guam and the AN/GRD-6 (HF/DF) system at Sidi Yahia. The combined systems enabled SOSUS to generate a submarine probability area (SPA). ASW operatives were then directed to the SPA to attempt to get in silent contact with the submarine. Initially, however, this sequence of events involved an inevitable time delay, adding somewhat to the task of locating and tracking the target submarine. There were other problems to overcome as well. Against diesel-electric submarines, the system was hampered by the fact that low-frequency tones were not emitted while the submarine was surfaced. The nuclear submarine, however, has numerous pieces of machinery supporting the operation of its nuclear reactor that are required to run at all times. In addition, their propeller designs created narrow-band tones that were a constant noise source while operating at sea, making them prime targets for SOSUS.

SOSUS also helped the Navy to highlight the signatures of the U.S. nuclear submarines. The results were astonishing. The most noted example was the Navy's first fully operational nuclear submarine, the USS *George Washington* (SSBN-598), as she undertook one of her first patrols in 1961. SOSUS stations on the East Coast of the U.S. tracked her during her entire trip across the Atlantic Ocean to England.

Another notable tracking achieved by SOSUS in 1962 took place when the SOSUS station in Barbados detected and tracked a Soviet Hotel-class submarine as it passed through the Greenland-Iceland-England area. SOSUS was also more than proving its value to the aviation-based ASW commands. ASW patrol aircraft were becoming more effective at tracking submarines, but further refinements were necessary. Submarine detections were being made at much longer ranges, so the area of location certainty for the target submarine was much larger than had been experienced before by the time an ASW aircraft arrived at the original detection point. This was primarily a problem when tracking diesel-electric submarines, as they would normally be surfaced for a finite period of time. Nuclear submarines, with their continuous noise signatures, made this problem much less significant.

This ability to detect and track Soviet submarines, almost at will, dramatically encouraged the Navy's acceptance of overall ASW operations as a complete complement to signals intelligence (SIGINT). Accordingly, in 1965 the Navy began installing SOSUS arrays in locations as close to the Soviet homeland as possible. They began by looking for locations where the USSR would have to travel sometimes lengthy distances to reach open-ocean patrol areas. For example, in order to reach the Atlantic from their primary nuclear submarine bases in the Black Sea, they would have to travel through the Mediterranean Sea's Strait of Gibraltar to reach the Atlantic.

An array was built in the Norwegian Sea in 1964 to search for Soviet submarines leaving their bases on the Kola Peninsula, and similar arrays were built in thirty-six locations around the world by 1981. What was so strategically and financially important to the U.S. was the fact that the nearly worldwide constant monitoring capability of the SOSUS arrays dramatically reduced the need for ships, submarines, and aircraft to maintain a barrier watch for USSR and its allies' submarines throughout the world. Furthermore, the U.S. was able to obtain rights from various countries in places like Keflavik, Iceland, and Rota, Spain, to construct bases in order to increase the U.S. proximity of ASW aircraft to Soviet shipping lanes. SOSUS also freed up U.S. attack submarines to be able to deploy in Soviet waters in order to conduct SIGINT gathering and to provide a first line of defense in case hostilities were to break out, as during the Cuban Missile Crisis in 1962.

The need for a permanent advanced-warning system against the threat of a submarine-based attack on the U.S. was clearly highlighted by the deployment of four Soviet Foxtrot-class submarines, equipped with nuclear missiles, to the Caribbean Sea during the Cuban Missile Crisis. During the crisis, SOSUS gave the U.S. the ideal combination of around-the-clock protection without alerting the USSR to the presence of a constant stream of responses in place by the U.S.

The 1970s saw the introduction of two significant threats to the ability of SOSUS to fulfill its early-warning detection role. The first, introduced in 1973, was the Soviet Delta-class ballistic-missile submarine. The second, introduced in 1978, was their Victor III SS-N. These two Soviet submarines were the first warning that the days of overwhelming U.S. ASW superiority over the USSR were coming to a close. What made the Delta so formidable to SOSUS was its submarine-launched ballistic missile (SLBM), which had sufficient range to reach the continental U.S. from waters in the vicinity of either the Barents Sea or the Sea of Okhotsk—approximately 3,900 miles and 4,300 miles, respectively—from the continental U.S.

We spent the next few days getting situated in our cubicle, undergoing a welcome-aboard physical (where we learned about the monthly "short arm" inspection), getting acclimated to our "watch section" (Section C), reviewing our duty assignment, and familiarizing ourselves with our "equipment." The only equipment change for me was a model upgrade on the R-390 military receiver, which we had used on Guam, to an R-390A model receiver. Other than that, the equipment I used for the next eighteen months was nearly identical to what I had used on Guam, which made for an easy transition to North Africa from the South Pacific environment. I was grateful for that.

For one thing, there would be no submarine TDA involved, although my assignments still revolved around Soviet submarine Morse code transmissions, primarily emanating from the

Black Sea and Odessa area. Ski's equipment was virtually unchanged, with the exception of minor antenna array variances for geographical reasons, much to his great pleasure. He'd been worrying about equipment changes ever since we left Guam back in November. In intelligence, nothing was more demanding than learning how to operate new DF and intercept equipment.

On the Soviet side, we learned about two significant changes in transmitter/receiver radio-intercept capability: their R-350M, which had been put into service earlier in the year, and the R-350 (Orel), which enabled them to engage a "burst" encoder in order to reduce the possibility of being intercepted, due to the extreme shortness of the radio transmission. This equipment had been put into play as a reconnaissance field radio for use as a portable guerrilla radio in battle zones or behind enemy lines. We learned later (in the spring of 1959) that this Soviet radio was more than likely used by opposing forces in the French-Algerian war, including by the French military, because the USSR had marketed the radio to several nations. It was also completely self-contained and lightweight, nearly identical to World War II German transmitter/receiver intercept radios. Because of the Orel's "burst" capability, my equipment was expanded to include a "recording device" to enable me to capture regular Morse code transmissions as well as the "burst" transmission at the same time.

Similar to the situation on Guam, our duty watch hours were EVE watch (1600–0000), DAY watch (0800–1600), and MID watch (0000–0800), followed by sixty-three hours off-duty. In reality, the Navy had done a good job in handling the transition from base to base with one exception: billets in the intelligence field. And that needs a bit of explanation. Because of the nature and secrecy of the work, you simply don't know anything at all about the guy sitting next to you, or underground, or in the field, or on a sub, or on an aircraft, or on a spy ship, or in the desert, or even in Washington with the National Security Agency. Much of the time you don't even know his name.

Think about it: During an eight-hour watch, sitting at your duty station in front of a bank of highly secret electronic equipment with a set of headphones on, you simply hardly notice his presence. And because of that fact, when you were off-duty, you usually spoke to, or otherwise communicated with, no one other than the three other guys in your cubicle in the barracks. You went on watch with them, went with them to the chow hall and to the gedunk, drank with them on liberty, and even went to get your monthly "short arm" inspection with them! The only exception was if you played on an organized sports team, such as football or basketball. And even then, you were lucky if you got an excuse for practice or a game if there was a conflict with your work schedule. I mean, with the exception of your cubicle mates, you hardly even remembered who the other twenty or so guys in your section were or why you all were there in the first place. It was no wonder that you'd occasionally punch some guy out, somewhere, sometime. Forget the buddy stuff. At least in the intelligence billets. On the other hand, you'd do anything for your cubicle mate, and he'd do the same. He was your brother.

So, to get on with the story, that first liberty in Port Lyautey about a week later was something else. We had gotten the afternoon bus to town, along with twenty to twenty-five other sailors in our winter blue uniforms. It was just Ski and me— we knew no one else on the bus—and like most similar bus rides in the Navy, there was near silence the entire forty or so minutes (night rides are different; most of the guys are drunk). The reason for the quiet was probably somewhat related to the fact that most of the guys on the bus were attached to Intelligence, not the ship's company. Anyway, when we got off the bus, we made a mental note of where we would catch the bus back to the base later that night, and we started out on our first liberty in Africa.

We spent some time just wandering around, then went into some French-owned shops and businesses, and before long found a bar that seemed to be attracting military types—some Air Force, Marines, and mostly Navy—which we knew from experience was a clear sign of trouble ahead. Three shore patrol guys outside the place proved the assumption to be correct. But this night wasn't going to be about one of our many fights. Not this time. Something different. And it wasn't "the girls."

We went inside. After wandering around for several minutes, we found two seats at one of the two bars in the place. One was all guys, the other probably an equal number of guys and girls. The girls looked to us to be French or other European—few if any other nationality—and they all looked intent on having a good time. We were sitting at the all-guys bar, so we had a good look at what was going on at the other bar, and I remember well that if you looked really hard, you could clearly see the beginnings of good times ahead from all the handwork underway! Unfortunately, because of what happened next, we never had the opportunity to visit with the girls. Not this night.

Ski and I started drinking Storck Beer, which we'd first tried in the gedunk the first night we were on the Sidi Yahia base, since it was the only beer sold on base[8] that was actually not bad at all. It wasn't long before I had to take a leak. After I tried to get a bartender's attention for several minutes, one of the sailors sitting next to me pointed out the way to the head, and I started on my way. The last thing I heard Ski say was "Don't get into any shit, 'cause I'm not coming to help you out." Well, I didn't start anything, and I'm certain it was because I really had to take a leak. Then.

---

8. It was a Moroccan-brewed beer, probably with some graft involved.

When I got to the entrance to the head—roughly a twelve-foot passageway into a room approximately twenty by twenty-five feet, all I could see were about fifteen to twenty men standing at the walls of the room, taking a leak into a trough on the floor running around the room, plus maybe six to eight men and women squatting down over holes in the floor in the middle of the room, some five feet or so apart—pants pulled down, skirts pulled up—taking a shit or otherwise relieving themselves. The holes in the floor were for number-two for the men, and for number-one and number-two for the women. *Whoa! What the hell have I gotten into now?* Piss over much of the floor, no toilet paper in evidence, and an ungodly stench that nearly put the poor camels to shame! Not entirely, but almost.

I moved my way to the wall, looked down at the narrow trench on the floor, kept my hands and everything else from touching anything, unbuttoned my pants, shut my eyes, and took a long piss, buttoned up, and got the hell out of there, almost tripping over the attendant's hose as he started to wash the room down or something like that. Welcome to the Third World. *Christ, what would I do if I had to take a shit? How would I balance myself? How would I keep my pants out of the all the piss and shit? GD, what the hell am I doing over here?*

Ski was still sitting at the bar, sipping his beer.

"How was it?" he asked.

"I'm not telling you nothing. Go see for yourself."

"What do you mean?"

"Just what I said, GD it. Go ahead, you'll see."

"You kidding me?"

"Would I kid you, Ski?"

"I'll be back in a minute."

"Yeah, I'll bet. Good luck. . . . By the way, Ski, pull your trousers up if you're just going to piss, or you'll get the cuffs wet."

"What did you say?"

"You heard me. I got mine all wet. Same with my shoes. Shit!"

Ski was back in a few minutes or so. Said he had to push some guy aside to get to the wall, and the whole damn floor was wet.

I told him, "That's the guy who hoses the place down."

All he said was "What guy?"

On our way out, Ski said, "Jesus, what do you do if you have to take a shit?"

I didn't say anything. I was still thinking about how to balance myself over that hole in the floor, and *Why wasn't there any toilet paper?* Ah, wonderful U.S. Navy. Wonderful North Africa. Thanks.

We walked out the door and back to the bus stop. A Moroccan was there with a basketful of fresh-baked, hot French bread. We both bought a loaf and got on the bus. At least the bread was good! We made it a habit from then on of buying a loaf every time we got the bus back to Sidi Yahia. Never got over how good it was. But after that first liberty and the bar, we damn sure didn't ask how they made it.

A week later we were underground at our duty station, doing principally the same work we'd done on Guam: tracking, monitoring, locating, and intercepting Soviet submarine radio transmissions operating in the Black Sea out of Odessa and from the area of Balaklava, not far from the port city of Sevastopol on the southern edge of Crimea, where Stalin had ordered the establishment and construction of a nuclear submarine base. The USSR had started construction of the base in 1957, not long before the launch of *Sputnik* in October of that year, amid the escalating Cold War between the U.S. and the USSR. The project was designed to be completed in four years, with secret submarine pens and corridors protected by concrete and steel-reinforced walls capable of withstanding a direct nuclear strike. Over 120,000 tons of rock was cut and removed from vast subterranean chambers open to the sea. Balaklava soon became one of the most secretive locations in the USSR and saw heavy use throughout the Cold War, working closely with the Soviet Black Sea Fleet, stationed at Sevastopol and Odessa; it was to play a critical part at the time of the Cuban Missile Crisis in October 1962.

When we left Guam in November 1957, the AN/FRD-10 CDAA was in its early planning and construction stage to prepare for Soviet implementation of the "burst" submarine radio transmission system in 1958, following the launch of *Sputnik*. In contrast, Sidi Yahia was utilizing an AN/GRD-6 (HF/DF) system, which was more than adequate for complementary intercept activity regarding the Black Sea operations of the USSR at Odessa, Balaklava, and Sevastopol. Of great significance as well, the AN/GRD-6 system was ideal for the activities taking place in Algeria, Morocco's eastern neighbor, which was engaged in the French-Algerian war.

That war, also called Algerian War of Independence (1954–1962), was waged to win Algerian independence from France.[9] The movement for independence had begun during World War I (1914–1918) and had gained momentum after French promises of greater self-rule in Algeria went unfulfilled after World War II (1939–1945).

In 1954 the National Liberation Front (in French, Front de libération nationale, or FLN) began a guerrilla war against France and sought diplomatic recognition at the U.N. to establish a sovereign Algerian state. Although Algerian fighters operated in the countryside—particularly along the country's borders—the most serious fighting took place in and around Algiers, where FLN fighters launched a series of violent urban attacks that came to be known as the Battle of Algiers (1956–1957).

---

9. The source for this paragraph and the next two is https://www.britannica.com/event/Algerian-War.

French forces (which increased to 500,000 troops) managed to regain control but only through brutal measures, and the ferocity of the fighting sapped the political will of the French to continue the conflict. In 1959 the French president, Charles de Gaulle, declared that the Algerians had the right to determine their own future. Despite terrorist acts by French Algerians opposed to independence and an attempted coup in France by elements of the French Army, an agreement was signed in 1962, and Algeria became independent.

At the time of our tour of duty, Naval Security Group–Sidi Yahia was classified as a hardship-duty station. Although it was a newly constructed base, built in 1953–1954, similar in design to the base on Guam (which had been constructed at the same time), it had no facilities for base personnel family-members housing, no base exchange, no hospital facilities other than a small clinic, no officers' or enlisted men's club for recreational purposes, no movie theater, and no commissary or other such amenities that most military bases, both in the U.S. and overseas, classified as standard base properties. Sidi Slimane Air Base, located about eighteen miles from our base, for example, provided full housing for dependents, a complete commissary, officers' and enlisted men's clubs, hospital facilities, and an indoor movie theater. What really got those of us at Sidi Yahia, however, was that even though it was a hardship-duty base, we still had a tour of duty of eighteen months to look forward to, while at Sidi Slimane the tour of duty was only twelve months.

What we did have, however, was an exceptionally active interservice varsity-level sports program, including basketball, baseball, and tackle football. Like we had done on Guam, Ski and I participated in the sports programs, especially tackle football. During the fall 1958 football season, we won the North African Division Conference Championship and participated in the Regional Championship game against Châteauroux-Déols Air Base in France. The game was played in the Santiago Bernabéu Stadium in the center of Madrid, Spain, home of the Real Madrid soccer team, before a pre-soccer match and over 40,000 fans who had no idea of what game we were playing. This site had been arranged by the State Department to introduce the French to American football. Unfortunately, for the second year, we lost. However, we both had a great time and fine memories that carried us forward into our days at Florida State in 1962–1965. Ski and I also participated in the intramural sports program, especially flag football, and enjoyed playing doubles tennis against officer and Marine guard teams.

We never forgot, however, that we were isolated from most of the world, surrounded by a mass of electrical and non-electrical fencing, guarded twenty-four hours a day by a Marine detachment and their dogs, in a rural area near the town of Sidi Yahia el Gharb, which was nothing more than a small meat and vegetable outdoor market with no electricity or refrigeration.

There was French bread and fruit, and we made weekly runs for both. There was also rumor of a French Foreign Legion post somewhere in the area, although we never saw or heard any evidence of it, with the exception of small-arms gunfire periodically, when our entire base would be under alert. And there was a Soviet radio-intercept station located about a mile or so from our base, near a mature orange grove that was off-limits to any of us.

In summary, at times it felt like we were incarcerated in a correctional facility, not a U.S. Naval Intelligence base. But I don't know anyone on the base during my tour of duty that really disliked Sidi Yahia. We were proud to be there, doing what we were doing, and it showed in our sports programs in particular and when we'd go on liberty to Port Lyautey or Rabat, and occasionally to Casablanca or Tangier. It's safe to say we collectively all felt we were the badasses of the Navy, with the toughest duty anywhere, and no one ever knew what it was that we did. And, as I said, we were proud of it, especially when we were on liberty.

The shore patrol knew who we were, and they didn't like us any more than any of the other military branches did, and that was just fine with us, especially when we met them on the football field or in a bar in town. They talk about shipboard duty, but this was a man's base, and we looked out for one another when on liberty, whether we knew you or not, be it in a bar, a nightclub, or—to be honest—even in a whorehouse. And there were more than one or two of them; Susan's in Casablanca and VCS ("Vine-Covered Shack") in Rabat, both dating back to World War II, were the best. Music, bar, dance floor, decor, food, and the girls. But let me tell you another story first.

In 1962, before attending Florida State University, I was working as the receiving dock manager at the Jordan Marsh department store in Fort Lauderdale. There was an old World War II vet who had a job running the baling room on the dock, where literally hundreds of empty boxes were dropped down a chute from the fourth-floor mark-up room. He'd bale them up and otherwise prepare them to be picked up later in the day. His name was Hugo, and he was a quiet, hardworking fellow, a retired U.S. Army sergeant with nearly thirty years of service. He'd been in the Allied invasion of North Africa in November of 1942—somewhere around Rabat and Casablanca, he said. He'd noticed the Navy cap I wore, which had the large word "NAVY" across the top, anchor in the middle, and stitched lettering below, indicating "South Pacific 1956–57" and "North Africa 1958–59." On the back, stitched in capital letters, was "VCS." He asked me about it, and about Rabat. I was dumbfounded and responded, "Yes, it was the 'Vine-Covered Shack' whorehouse." He laughed and said he'd been there back when he was in Africa during World War II, to which I replied something to the effect that "Well, the girls were probably the same ones you'd met!" I told him that the

Navy and the Moroccan government were still supervising and inspecting them in the late 1950s and that the Navy went a step further with a required short-arm inspection every month.

We did have a chapel on base, because there were times when you needed to speak with the chaplain, especially about matters such as this as well as other matters back home. And there were a lot of issues, mostly about girlfriends and family matters, however. No matter where you go, there you are.

My favorite song at the time of my military service (and even today) was Caterina Valente's "The Breeze and I" in 1958. It was my favorite because of the song itself, the quality of the artist as an international singer from Italy with a world-renowned status, and two intertwined events I experienced involving her. The first during a MID watch at work in North Africa and the second in Gibraltar.

I was on the MID watch at Sidi Yahia, Morocco, in late November 1958, copying a Soviet diplomatic radio transmission from Moscow to their consulate office in Goa (a former Portuguese province annexed by India in 1961). I was on a frequency-change search when suddenly I came in contact with a Marine shortwave voice transmission originating in the Indian Ocean from an English-speaking guy, sailing alone, he had said, aboard his sloop on his way to the Seychelles from Goa. There was music in the background. Some filtering and other "adjustments" later, and I heard what at the time I felt was the most incredible female voice I had ever heard. She was singing about a love affair and "the breeze and I." I listened until it was over, then got back to my job. I couldn't get that song out of my mind, though. Nor could I get out of my mind how it had all evolved. And where it had come from. On a small sloop, in the middle of the Indian Ocean, a guy sailing alone. Accompanied by music.

All I knew was that I wanted to hear the singer and the recording again. And I got a chance. Pure luck. I would see her in person in Gibraltar in a concert on the beach in the very near future. In fact, a week later, she would start the concert on a pedestal rising from the orchestra pit in the center of the nightclub. And it would begin with "The Breeze and I." I would be in the presence of one of the world's greatest singers. This was shortly after Thanksgiving 1958 and our football team's trip to Madrid to play for the Regional Championship against an Air Force team from Châteauroux-Déols Air Base, France (we lost).

Here was a second trip we took to Gibraltar: Ski said to me, "You know, all the time we've been in the Navy, I've never sent Christmas presents back home." I said something snide like "What, you think you're Santa Claus or something?" Ski immediately said something I can't repeat here, but right away I knew we were going to go up to Gibraltar and buy Christmas presents. This was not up for discussion. I remembered the knife shop on Main Street, china and linen shops that had the stuff Mom and Grandmother Alexander would love, and then there was the Rock Hotel, the oldest and best on Gibraltar, with—in my opinion—the best restaurant. Especially the seafood and my favorite, grilled swordfish. I was glad we would be going back again.

"I'm ready," I said. "Give me some scrip, and I'll get us on the next 'fluce run.'" A "fluce run" is a military term for exchanging military scrip, our form of pay, for local currency when you're stationed in a foreign country. I'm sure it was illegal, but the brass on our base never enforced it. Ski gave me $150 in military scrip; I added mine, and we started inquiring as to who would be making the next "fluce run" and when. Usually two or more off-duty guys had access to, or owned, a vehicle. They'd charge a "commission" of 5 percent to cover their costs for the exchange with some contact in Tangier and return with French francs, Spanish pesetas, and/or English pounds, whatever it was you wanted. Incidentally, the purchaser of the scrip or his agent would take the scrip into Europe, where it would be exchanged for different types of currencies at predetermined "exchange rates," or it would be used directly in one of the U.S. military base exchanges for U.S. products of all sorts. See how much you can learn in the military? Learn all about international finance, economics, monetary policy, and on and on—all without reading or studying a textbook of any kind. Just another Navy benefit from the old-timers, not the officers! And another thing: If you were planning on visiting "Susan's" in Casablanca or "VCS" in Rabat for the night, you didn't even have to pay with French francs; you just paid for your "purchase" with a "mil," the French equivalent in military scrip to a thousand French francs, or about the going rate for an "all-nighter" ($10). Not bad, huh?

So with all that taken care of, we got our tennis rackets and headed out to the courts! Man, life was tough in the Navy, all the way over there in North Africa with nothing to do! Neither of us had the slightest idea what was about to happen on the way to Tangier Friday night. But neither of us would ever forget it either.

Late in the afternoon in early December 1958, after missing the last train to Tangier from Port Lyautey, Ski and I boarded a bus instead on the inland route to Tangier and then on to Gibraltar to do some Christmas shopping. Originally, our plan had been to take the afternoon train that day along the Atlantic coast from Port Lyautey to Tangier in time to catch the last ferry, the *Mons Calpe*, to Gibraltar, which left around 1900 every day for the fifty-minute cruise. We knew from past experience and from other guys on our base who had taken the train that the scenic coastal route to Tangier was roughly an hour shorter than the inland bus route. We'd also been told it was a lot safer. We soon found out that the local bus we boarded would result in a trip to hell.

Gibraltar is a British Overseas Territory that occupies a narrow peninsula of Spain's southern Mediterranean coast, northeast of the Strait of Gibraltar. Located on the southern end of the Iberian Peninsula, it shares its northern border with Spain, and the Rock of Gibraltar is its major landmark. Gibraltar is largely inhabited by Spanish and British residents, but there are also Portuguese, German, and Maltese influences as well as Moroccan and Indian. English is the official language, and it is prevalent in all aspects of life in Gibraltar, from government to commerce, to education and the media. Gibraltar is home to over five hundred plant species and the Barbary macaque monkey, which is the only wild monkey found in Europe. From 1958 to 1959, there was only one ferry service to and from Tangier and Gibraltar, serving both ports with six or more trips daily. There's currently no ferry service between Tangier and Gibraltar; however, Royal Air Maroc and British Airways have several flights daily, and ferry service is available from Algeciras, Spain, to Gibraltar throughout the day.

But back to our story that fateful day in December 1958. We knew that by taking the bus, we'd have to spend the night in Tangier, since it was a nearly four-hour bus trip on the back roads as opposed to the train in less than two hours. Instead of spending the night at the Rock Hotel in Gibraltar, we'd be sleeping on a bench in the Tangier bus station and catching the 0700 ferry to Gibraltar the next morning. But that would be possible only if we were successful in getting to Tangier by 2100, when the bus station closed. After 2100 we'd have to find a place to sleep at the police station jail, and we really wanted to avoid that if at all possible. We'd involuntarily been there before about six months earlier, and the event still bothered us. The jail had one large holding room, no furniture, no water, and one partial bathroom. We'd spent the night—four of us from our base at Sidi Yahia—fighting off drunks, pickpockets, you-know-whats, and beggars looking for anything they could steal if you fell asleep. Or you could be drawn into a fight while someone took your travel belongings.

The reason we had everything with us as we traveled was simply because we'd been warned that if we asked to store our stuff with the admitting personnel, that would be the last time we would see it, because in the morning, the shift would change—and with the night shift would go all of our belongings! All this and the fact that the only bathroom facility in the room was the trough along one wall and that there were roughly fifty people in the room at any given time. And always with us was the smell of feces, urine, and vomit.

With that said, the last places we knew for sure we'd be staying if we missed the ferry were (1) the bus station, (2) the police station, or (3) outside the locked office of the ferryboat service. And with just the two of us, we knew it wouldn't be outside the locked offices of the ferryboat service. What about a hotel room, you ask? No such thing after 2100 unless you had a reservation and were willing to pay triple rates.

What really bothered us this minute was that by missing an earlier bus that traveled the coastal route to Tangier, which was more like an express bus, the only service we had available to us at this time was the "local" bus. And that was what we were on. Our bus was full with local-stop travelers, mostly Arab women with babies or small children, as well as chickens in cages either in the bus or on top, among the baggage and other animals, including an occasional goat in a cage. Also on top of the bus were auto parts, auto tires, and miscellaneous junk of all sorts. Inside the bus was almost as bad, and we placed our travel bags on the floor in front of our seat. Once again, the stench was ungodly. But little did we know that shortly after we left the station and we were out into the hills and valleys, this trip would become a nightmare.

The route took us eastward and then northward through any number of small villages and towns, as well as numerous stops alongside the road to board and discharge passengers.

Then came the numerous stops to enable passengers to relieve themselves along the roadway. Soon we were out in the country. The roads were already in poor condition, but the farther we progressed, the worse they got, until they appeared to be full of potholes and road junk every inch of the way.

Halfway into what soon became a four-hour trip (we were still facing at least two more hours to Tangier, with an estimated arrival time of between 2030 and 2100), in an area of small hills and valleys, one of the few automobiles or trucks we'd seen since leaving Port Lyautey suddenly passed us at a high rate of speed—half on and half off the road. It swerved back in front of the bus and flashed its brake lights as it came to a screeching halt. The bus driver tried to avoid a collision by running off the road and nearly crashing into a stand of small trees growing along the side.

Before we could see what the hell was going on, many of the passengers were screaming and attempting to grab their children and move to the rear of the bus. Three Arabs or Algerian guerrillas with their heads and faces covered had boarded the bus. They were carrying rifles and what looked to me like a World War II German Luger, and they started screaming in a mixture of Arabic and something else neither Ski nor I recognized; they were waving their weapons around wildly. Both of us recalled that the Marines guarding our base in Sidi Yahia had instructed us on what we should do if we ever faced such a situation. We should place our hands on the back of the seat in front of us and look directly at the terrorists. We should keep our eyes concentrated on their eyes at all times—without ever looking away. The noise and commotion inside the bus was overpowering, to say the least, and it got worse each time one of the terrorists raised or waved his weapon at one of the passengers, including us. Still, keep your eyes on the terrorist. Constantly. Yeah, easier said than done, buddy, I thought, and I'm sure Ski felt the same way.

Then both Ski and I saw the terrorist with the German

Luger suddenly lunge at a nondescript Moroccan or Algerian gentleman sitting by a window halfway behind a woman holding a baby. She frantically screamed and grasped the baby close. The terrorist jabbed the Luger in the man's face, yelled something to him in Arabic (I guess), grabbed him by the shoulder, and jerked him up violently from his seat. Immediately, one of the two other terrorists joined him, grabbing the hostage's other shoulder and pulling him to the aisle of the bus, where the third terrorist continued to threaten the passengers with his rifle, jabbing it in their faces.

Without much fanfare, the three terrorists and their hostage moved to the door of the bus and exited, firing at least one rifle into the air as they quickly entered their vehicle and drove away, leaving only a choking dust cloud. The woman who had been sitting next to the victim continued to cry hysterically, while several other women attempted to console her. It was dark, cold, and deserted ahead—no one else on the road. Was this over?

Ski and I looked at each other, stunned, to say the least. Finally, he said, "That jarhead on the base was right. . . . Still can't believe what just happened."

"You and me both, Ski," I replied.

Wasn't a bad trip from then on, but it was a trip neither of us ever forgot. We never heard anything more about the assault on the bus. And when we finally did arrive in Tangier after 2100, the bus station was still open—no doubt because of what had happened earlier. They allowed us and several other passengers to stay inside, sleeping on benches. At 0700 the next morning, we were on our way to Gibraltar—with all the bad memories.

It was in the early afternoon the next day when Ski and I arrived back in Port Lyautey in time for our EVE watch at 1600. But we still had one event ahead of us. We were tired, mentally and physically, after the preceding two days, and we attributed it to our experience on the bus when we were facing our first confrontation. We firmly believed this experience was probably one that thousands of guys had faced during wartime: coming face to face with the possibility of death. Not pleasant, believe me, and the feeling has remained with me all my life. Much like on the submarine while stationed on Guam, and a leak somewhere around the forward torpedo room led me to believe the sub was sinking and I was on it—some 400 feet under the surface of the Pacific, in the Mariana Trench, 36,000 feet deep. Something had happened to me at that time, because in 2017, after a surgical event and amputation during which I was sedated, I came out of anesthesiology in the presence of my doctors, talking about "drowning at sea" some sixty years earlier.

Shortly after arriving at Sidi Yahia back in 1958, during our orientation, the Marine duty officer gave a brief speech, during which he welcomed us new guys to the realities of being assigned to a hazardous-duty station (Morocco during the French-Algerian war, 1954–1962)—specifically "guerrilla warfare" activities, including what we had just witnessed on our bus ride. Most of his remarks involved attempts by guerrilla units attempting to breach the base, searching for weapons, vehicles, copper, and miscellaneous equipment, etc. These attempts happened two or three times a month, based, we guessed, on how the war was going. The base Marine guard unit generally responded to these security breaches by releasing a goodly number of their forty German shepherds and letting them run out. Our base had it significantly better than the French Foreign Legion base, about three miles down the road. They got breached weekly.

The duty officer also mentioned the occasional guerrilla attempt to stop vehicles and buses, board them, and rob or harass drivers and passengers, much like we had just seen. Specifically, his advice back when we had first arrived at the base was to "comply with their instructions, keep your hands clearly in view, and look them in the eyes." Well, we had taken his advice, and it had all worked out well for us. He had also told us that we were to report any such activity we experienced that involved contact with guerrillas or similar situations.

We told the duty officer of our experience and that his earlier advice of placing our hands on the seat in front of us if on a bus and looking the attackers in the eye while being detained had worked well for us, as we had not been harmed or asked for anything during the event. He filled out an incident report, we both signed it, and we headed for our barracks to get ready for the EVE watch. Just another day in Naval Intelligence.

Little did we know that both Ski and I would, in the near future, be on a TDA in the Sahara Desert, involved, albeit in an indirect way, in the French-Algerian war.

It was roughly 0700 to 0730, February 3, 1959, and Section C was ending up the MID watch, when our watch officer told us to shut down our equipment momentarily. All of us were shocked. What the hell was this? I was just about set to bring up Odessa for their morning transmission. It was only a moment later that he said he had something he wanted us to listen to. Before I even had another thought, all I could hear was Buddy Holly singing "Peggy Sue." There wasn't any other sound in the room—no typewriters, no teletypes, nothing but the music. He turned down the sound and told us, "Buddy Holly, Ritchie Valens, and the Big Bopper had all been killed in a plane crash near Clear Lake, Iowa, after performing a 'Winter Dance Party' concert at the Surf Ballroom."

Not a word was spoken as one by one we listened to "That'll Be the Day," "Rave On!" and "Peggy Sue"—all that great music of the 1950s. And my all-time favorite, "Oh Boy!" Within a minute, virtually all radio receivers were tuned to the New York or Chicago station playing Buddy Holly's songs in tribute. Here we were, more than 4,200 miles away, underground, listening to some of the greatest 1950s music, while at the same time, some were dancing, some crying, at our stations. Ritchie Valens's "La Bamba" and the Big Bopper's "Chantilly Lace" boomed into the room. Where were you *the day the music died?*

Truly a memorable day in my life. About twenty minutes later, the DAY watch guys entered and were stunned. They'd been to chow and were completely unaware of the situation. Back in the '50s, the early days of rock 'n' roll, musicians were as big as anything else in any teen's life, and one of the most popular was Buddy Holly. Three years later, when Ski and I reunited at Florida State University after completing our tour of duty with the Navy, the Righteous Brothers came out with "You've Lost That Lovin' Feelin'," a song that became the most played 45 rpm in the history of blues and rock 'n' roll. It also became the most favorite song for both Ski and me, and it immediately took us back to that day in February 1959 when we'd learned of Buddy Holly's death.

It wasn't long after that day that Ski and I were called into the NSG commander's office, where we learned that we'd both be together on "special missions," a temporary duty assignment in the Sahara Desert, conducting certain SIGINT duties relating to guerrilla and French military communications. Other than that, we'd learn more from our evaluator, who would accompany us on each mission. He gave the particulars for the missions—primary and secondary equipment, etc., and when the missions would commence; then he wished us well.

Our only thought after this meeting was *What the hell was this all about?* Ski was especially concerned, and all I could do was recall my TDA on Guam back in 1957, in the Mariana Trench—one that I had no fond memories of, believe me. I felt a lot better about this TDA.

EIGHT

ODESSA AND THE BLACK SEA

When Ski and I finally acclimated ourselves to our new base, learned our assignment, familiarized ourselves with certain equipment and duties, and got our watch section, some of the guys told us a story about the existence of a covert World War II German radio-intercept station located under an abandoned chalet in Ifrane, an Alpine winter resort of sorts built by the French in the Middle Atlas Mountains somewhere around the late 1930s. It was located approximately 140 miles east of Casablanca, which back in the early days of World War II, before the Allied invasion of French North Africa in November 1942, housed a small garrison of German troops stationed there. From Sidi Yahia el Gharb, the distance was approximately 85 miles east.

The chalet, a two-and-a-half-story residence similar in construction to many ski-resort homes and villas, was located roughly a mile from the village of Ifrane in a rough, forested area with dense conifers and heavy shrubs. Chalets in this area of the mountains were generally constructed on large plots approximately a quarter mile apart, among a grouping of two or three other such properties. The chalet itself, although completely abandoned, was still in relatively good condition, probably in part because of the weather and climate. But the interior had been completely ransacked, no doubt by marauding Berbers during the warmer summer months of the year, when the only hotel, the Grand, was closed, as were most of the other commercial businesses.

Berbers are an ethnic group indigenous to North Africa.[10] They are distributed in an area stretching from the Atlantic Ocean to the Siwa Oasis in Egypt, and from the Mediterranean Sea to the Niger River. Berber history goes back to prehistoric times. They've been around for at least four thousand years or maybe more. Calling themselves Amazigh, the proud raiders, they fought against the Romans, the Arabs, and the French invaders. Even though the Romans and others have tried to colonize the Berber people, they have managed to preserve their own language and culture, and in reality, they were never beaten!

A light-skinned people, they have been called by many names: Libyans by the ancient Greeks, Numidians and Africans by the Romans, and Moors by medieval Europeans. In fact, it was the Arabs who came up with the *Berber* name. Islam came to the Berbers in the eighth and ninth centuries. Prior to then, most Berbers across Africa were Christian or Jewish. Two great Islamic Berber dynasties, the Almoravids and the Almohads, ruled large parts of Spain and northwest Africa.

Berbers are often portrayed as nomadic people crossing the desert on camels, but most are farmers in the mountains and valleys throughout northern Africa. Some do trade throughout the region, however. Historically, Berber merchants were responsible for transporting goods by camel caravans. There were basically five trans-Saharan trade routes, which extended across the Sahara from the Mediterranean

10. The source for this paragraph and the next three is https://www.morocco-ecotours.com/berber-history/.

coast of Africa to the great cities situated on the southern edge of the Sahara, such as Timbuktu in Mali. From the northern terminus the goods were distributed throughout the world.[11]

Most of the 27 million Moroccans are either Berbers, Arabs, or Moors (people of Berber-Arab descent). Most of today's Berbers live in the mountains of Morocco while the Arabs and Moors live in the cities, though it is very common these days to see Berbers running, owning, and operating small shops and other commercial endeavors.

Virtually all the chalets in Ifrane were vacant during the hottest months of the summer, and at this time there was very little snow in the area. This, of course, was in the late 1950s. Today, however, it is a thriving summer and winter resort area, complete with several new hotels and an English-language liberal-arts curriculum college named Al Akhawayn University.

The chalet appeared to have been built on top of the German radio-intercept station, more than likely intentionally. Despite the sketchy directions we'd received back on base, we were able to locate the chalet and, after a short search, the entrance to the radio station: a low-ceilinged tunnel about three feet wide by six feet high, roughly one hundred feet away from the radio station itself. Clues that a once-existing metal entrance door still remained in the ten or so hinges buried in the poured-concrete entrance doorway. The tunnel was built under a relatively steep slope away from the chalet, and it joined up to the radio station roughly six feet below the sloped surface and exterior wall of the chalet.

The interior structures of the radio station walls were built of steel-bar-reinforced concrete roughly three feet thick, with a roof approximately four feet thick of the same material. The

---

11. The goods from Timbuktu reached Europe from modern-day Morocco, Algeria, and Tunisia. See, for example, https://en.wikipedia.org/wiki/Sijilmasa.

entire area was about twenty by thirty feet. There were several vents located in the walls where a bathroom and small chow hall area had once been. We also noted several small holes in the ceiling of the radio room, which appeared to have been conduits of some sort to the living room and dining room of the chalet. Somewhat of a mystery to us, however, was the apparent lack of electrical outlets throughout the room. Finally, there was evidence of two small rooms, perhaps six by nine feet, as well as shelving around the entire room— more than likely where different sorts of radio transmitting/ receiving equipment had been installed. The walls were bare concrete with very little remaining signs of having been painted, but they were virtually covered by layers of graffiti, much of it in French and Arabic with a smattering of English, including some from CTs at our base at Sidi Yahia and the U.S. Naval Radio Transmitter Communications Station at Bouknadel.

There was an eerie feeling in the room. It probably came from our flashlights reflecting all around the room. Although we tried to keep them focused on one area at a time, we each gathered our thoughts about what we were seeing. Not more than sixteen years before, Field Marshal Erwin Rommel himself might have been in this place. He had, in fact, been in Casablanca earlier, invited by the Vichy regime, before the Allied invasion of North Africa in November 1942. We'd studied Rommel and German communications intelligence at Imperial Beach, and here we were thinking that maybe Rommel himself stood in the very spot we were standing, among German communications intelligence operatives like ourselves. In fact, the very size of the room spoke to its importance, and we realized that it must have played a significant part during the early portion of the German campaign in North Africa.

We never went back to the site. Kindred souls, perhaps?

After we left Ifrane, one of the guys suggested that we go see the site of Volubilis, the Roman Empire ruins located near the city of Meknes, around forty miles from Ifrane and on the way back to Sidi Yahia. The closest city to the ruins was the village of Moulay Idriss, a picturesque place near the Fertassa River, which also ran on one side of Volubilis and added quite a bit of tranquility to the ruins. None of us had ever seen historical ruins of any type, so we thought it was a good idea.

It did not take us long to get to Moulay Idriss, where we picked up some information about the place in a small shop located at the entrance to the village. It seems that Volubilis was described in its early days as a colony; it had been an Athenian settlement since the third century BC. We also learned that the Romans had transformed it into a typical city, complete with mansions to house the Roman officials, a town center, a triumphal arch, and temples devoted to the gods.

Christianity was later the practiced religion, and Latin was the language spoken by the Greeks, Jews, and Syrians who lived in Volubilis at the time. The lands there still produced numerous commodities that were common in its early days, such as grains and olive oil, which were then exported to Rome. Finally, Volubilis was the final stop of the Roman imperial road that went across France, Spain, and down from Morocco's northern city of Tangier to Volubilis, which is located in the mid-central area of Morocco.

Volubilis was abandoned by the Romans after the fall of the Western Roman Empire in the fifth century AD. We were totally surprised when we finally arrived at the ruins. There was no sign whatsoever of human life anywhere near the place—no "tourist" center, no caretakers, no guards, no one at all. Just the four of us, and we were free to explore the entire site, from the archways and columns, fountains and the aqueduct, to the baths. As we approached the site, we could see all of these ruins as well as the lush green plateau upon which Volubilis sat, together with a massive expanse of cypress trees among the columns and arches.

It really was an exciting place to visit, even from a Navy

enlisted man's perspective. We probably spent an hour or so just wandering around. In the fading light around 1800 hours, when we visited, it had a mystical, surreal feel. Today, the site has been substantially restored and developed as a tourist destination. There is also an annual concert held in June among the ancient ruins at Volubilis, called the "Festival of World Sacred Music," which is attended by tourists from around the world.

We'd had enough history and culture in one day to last a lifetime, from the German World War II signals intelligence to the Roman Empire and its influence on Morocco, and to be truthful, we were glad to get back to Sidi Yahia.

Yes, we were more than anxious to get back to our job as signals intelligence operatives, in the Cold War between the U.S. and the USSR. Soon we'd be on the front lines here in Africa, far from the tranquil splendor of the South Pacific and its own unique set of situations facing the country. In addition to submarines in the Black Sea, we were dealing with an ally and her battle with Algeria in the French-Algerian war, and it wasn't pretty, nor was it going to get better anytime soon. The rest of our country might not have known about the reality of the Cold War, but we knew the relationship between the world's most important military powers was as dangerous as any "war" could have ever been.

The meaning of "war" had changed, and we knew it all too well. Instead of war between two or more nations, the world—although hardly anyone realized it at this early date—was past that point. The real issue was the survival of mankind. But did anyone realize it? I think maybe *we* did. And that's why it frightened us so. The stakes were getting higher and higher.

Balaklava had functioned as an active naval port for centuries, although the Soviet submarine base was not constructed until 1957, when the USSR issued a directive to establish a fleet of nuclear submarines in the Black Sea. It was constructed in a manner to be invisible from prying eyes, and the project took nearly four years to complete. Over 120,000 tons of rock were cut and removed from vast, subterranean chambers open to the waters of the Black Sea. The removal was made at night on barges under conditions of complete secrecy. The complex also included the repair and technical base, designed for the storage and maintenance of nuclear weapons. The temperature inside the base was about fifteen degrees.

At the time of its completion, sometime around 1960, the USSR claimed that the submarine base was virtually indestructible. The secret submarine pens and corridors were protected by a shell of concrete and steel capable of surviving a nuclear strike of up to one hundred kilotons, making the base one of the most secure in the entire world. According to a Ukraine website on military history, the submarine base was built for hiding, repairing, and maintaining submarines as well as for the storage of ammunition for these submarines. The channel of the facility could accommodate seven nuclear submarines.

The Balaklava submarine base saw heavy duty throughout the Cold War, including during the Cuban Missile Crisis of 1962. In fact, the placing of PGM-19 Jupiter medium-range ballistic missiles (MRBMs) in Turkey by the U.S. provoked the USSR to respond directly with nuclear-armament activities in Cuba and—in anticipation of an imminent U.S. attack on Cuba (or on the USSR from Turkey)—to scramble their nuclear-powered submarines from Balaklava to the waters between Cuba and the U.S. The Soviet buildup of its submarine force in the 1950s and early 1960s was centered in the Black Sea in two Ukraine ports: the USSR's largest port at Odessa and the home port of the USSR's Black Sea Fleet at Sevastopol.

As a SIGINT intercept operative specializing in Soviet submarine traffic in the South Pacific originating at Vladivostok, USSR, I was on Watch Section C here at Sidi Yahia el

Gharb, Morocco, North Africa. My assignment was to monitor
Soviet submarine traffic at the recently discovered, highly
secret Soviet naval facility at Balaklava, Ukraine, in the Black
Sea, just south of Odessa, a major Soviet submarine base on
the Black Sea. Beginning in 1956, the USSR had undertaken
the construction of highly classified nuclear submarines of
the 658 class (the Hotel class). These submarines were
entirely constructed at the Balaklava facility as a major element of the USSR's emphasis on submarines as its primary
offensive nuclear weapons force. In 1958, the construction
and deployment of these submarines included the newest
R-13 SLBM. This missile was capable of being launched from
beneath the sea, from these nuclear-powered submarines,
which were "silent," compared with earlier models and World
War II submarines that were conventionally powered and
equipped. Accordingly, they were to play a critical role in the
Cuban Missile Crisis of 1962, when a pack of six such submarines were detected by the U.S. Navy roughly six hundred to
seven hundred miles north of the flotilla of some forty or so
Soviet ships approaching Cuba. That flotilla was carrying
what was purported to be cargoes of missile parts and com-
ponents for the final construction of a battalion of
short-to-middle-range guided-missile facilities already underway in Cuba. These six submarines had secretly embarked
from the Balaklava-Odessa area sometime around early
October 1962, and they had been detected and tracked by
the Navy from its intelligence base at Sidi Yahia and the
Naval base at Rota, Spain, once they entered the Mediterranean Sea.

As an experienced ASW intercept operative with the
knowledge of both offensive and defensive Soviet submarine
weapons as well as U.S. Navy counter-weapons and surveillance devices, I knew that Sidi Yahia watch stations had been
on standby alert for several weeks and were finally activated
in early October 1962.

While the U.S. had focused its SIGINT activities on the fact that its defensive system considered the Soviet submarines—initially at least—as defensive weapons of war, we knew many were capable of becoming offensive weapons at any time. Accordingly, the U.S. Navy's primary ASW defense systems focused upon surveillance and detection of Soviet submarines and the protection of the U.S. from any aggression by the USSR in the event of a full-out nuclear war. Therefore, the U.S. was well equipped to counter any Soviet offensive attack.

Substantial progress in ASW had been undertaken and success achieved through such programs as SOSUS and White Cloud throughout the world. We were successful, even though the USSR had been successful in eliminating the fatal flaws that had existed by virtue of the power systems they had initially employed before the development and implementation of nuclear-powered submarines. For example, the fatal flaw of earlier submarines was their conventional power. Electric- and fossil-fuel-powered propulsion systems made them completely vulnerable to detection simply because their power systems could not be "silenced." As a result, they could be monitored by conventional detection systems, which initially had included limitations based on distance. An "unsilenced" submarine could be detected and tracked by the U.S. anywhere and anytime by SOSUS. And, as we discussed earlier, SOSUS came into play immediately after the USSR launched *Sputnik* in 1957 and subsequently changed its method of communications with submarines to the "burst" method of communication.

NINE

SAHARA DESERT

The French-Algerian war (November 1, 1954, to March 19, 1962) evolved out of nationalism efforts of Algeria's neighbor, French Morocco, and its citizens, dating back to 1920, to gain its independence from France. From the 1920s until roughly 1943 during World War II, the French were able to contain these nationalistic trends among the populist movements, but in 1944 Moroccan nationalists formed the Istiqlal Party (or Independent Party), which challenged colonialism. In response, the French arrested all the leaders of the Istiqlal Party, accusing them of working and supporting the Germans. Conflict between Moroccan nationalists and the French government continued into the 1950s. In December 1952, riots broke out in Casablanca, Morocco's largest city. The riots led to the banning by the Moroccan government of the Istiqlal Party and the Moroccan Communist Party. Further actions against the Moroccan government by the French led to Moroccan revolts in the form of terrorist acts and armed movements. Finally, in March 1956, after forty-four years of colonization, Morocco finally gained its independence. In Algeria, the stage had been set for what soon became the French-Algerian war, which broke out in November 1954.

There were more than thirty attempts on the life of General Charles de Gaulle, more than on any other military general's life in history. There was also a planned assassination in the spring of 1959 that has never been revealed—until now. It was planned by, and included the involvement of, one of the highest-ranking generals in the French Army, Raoul Salan, and a colonel in the French Air Force, Jean-Marie Bastien-Thiry. This is the story behind that planned assassination plot and my part in thwarting it.

Ski and I had spent most of our time in North Africa tracking, monitoring, locating, and intercepting Soviet diplomatic CW radio traffic between Moscow and the Black Sea area, including the countries of Bulgaria, Romania, Turkey, Hungary, Ukraine, and the Soviet naval bases at Odessa, Balaklava, and Sevastopol. In January 1959, we had also begun to search the lower frequencies for evidence of guerrilla radio communications in and around Algeria during the French-Algerian war.

It was a pisser. Keeping up with our assignment was at first extremely difficult on the Sahara Desert. That desert, covering most of North Africa, is the largest desert in the world; from north to south, the Sahara is between 800 and 1,200 miles, and it is at least 3,000 miles from east to west.

Increasingly, we were given certain data and information from our evaluator involving specific frequency targets and geographical locations. Several weeks later, we were on a TDA that involved—for a short period—daily flights on a Navy RD4 (civilian DC-3) especially equipped and camouflaged. It had large inflated tires for use on camel trails and similar such landing areas. We flew out of Sidi Slimane Air Base, about twenty miles east from our base. We'd usually leave about 0400 hours, fly over the Middle Atlas Mountains, and put down on old camel trails on the Sahara Desert in Algerian territory. This site had been determined "best" geographically and otherwise for an intercept mission.

In an assignment such as this, we were somewhere

between the small Algerian town of Béchar and the Moroccan border, set up under the wing of our camouflaged RD4 nestled in some camel tracks. It was just Ski and myself, along with the pilot and co-pilot—and the evaluator, of course, who was a Naval officer (lieutenant junior grade) attached to Naval Intelligence. He was a challenge, and by design, we never knew his name. Every half hour or so, he would leave the comfort of the plane, walk over to where we were working, look at our work product, take what he wanted, and go back to the plane, where he would transmit certain of our work product back to our base at Sidi Yahia or, if he deemed it necessary, to Bouknadel, the intelligence transmitter site in Morocco, for—under certain circumstances—direct transmission to Washington, D.C. That was our evaluator's primary responsibility.

We didn't know what we were searching for, but we soon found out. Ski and I were starting to do a fairly decent job of keeping up with the situation, whether it was all encrypted communications or open-com (non-encrypted), as was the case in much guerrilla CW communication transmissions to or from French Algerian Muslim units fighting the war.

Just me, Ski, two aircraft crew members, and our evaluator, who spoke, read, and wrote French and Arabic fluently. And, of course, our escort and cover for the trips: a Convair B-58 Hustler from Sidi Slimane Air Base and its crew of three: a pilot, a navigator, and a defense systems (weapons) operator, whose presence came in handy on more than one occasion. The B-58 was some aircraft. Holder of numerous world speed and altitude records, armed with a 20 mm cannon and nuclear and non-nuclear weapons in pods of under-wing pylons, it had a maximum speed in excess of 1,300 miles per hour and a ceiling over 65,000 feet. We never did know why we needed that much fly power for our mission, but on the other hand, we were grateful for it. We were aware of many Cold War Navy "spy planes" (such as ours) that had been shot down with loss of life while we were stationed on Guam.

I still today don't know who or why our superiors figured out that it would be a good idea for us to try to conduct our hunter-gatherer work out on the Sahara Desert instead of back on the base in Sidi Yahia. Anyway, it always seemed to come down to something like the TDA on Guam in the submarines, in the Mariana Trench, listening for Soviet submarines and humpback whale calls.

Our evaluator explained that the reason we had to conduct our intercept work in the Sahara Desert was, among other things, related to the fact that the Middle and High Atlas Mountains lay directly between our base and the area in Algeria where we would be conducting our search. Simply put, in order to improve the quality of the intercept, we had to be on the other side of the mountains. In addition to the geophysical conditions, there were other factors that could be a problem for our intercept work. Namely: the anticipated communications equipment the Algerian rebels were using and the location of their transmitting bases. These factors contributed to our ability to gather the communications we needed to confirm transmissions and to develop triangulation positions to enable us to pinpoint a transmitter's physical location. Excuse me for the "double talk." Important? I'll say.

For example, years later, in the Vietnam War, SIGINT incurred similar "problems" that materially impacted our ability to obtain significant quantities of quality CW radio and other communications necessary to conduct this type of war. Both the Viet Cong and the People's Army of Vietnam employed guerrilla tactics concerning troop movements and strategic positions. The use of HF/DF in Vietnam was vital in waging a war of basically guerrilla warfare tactics. Today this type of "war" (similar to the one waged with "ISIS") is hard enough as it is, since it is conducted by numerous groups of guerrilla units with small-arms weapons, as opposed to much larger, heavily equipped units and men with tanks, etc., much like those in World War I and World War II.

Guerrilla warfare in Algeria, like that in Vietnam, was driven by low-frequency, CW Morse code, subject to varying environmental and geographical conditions that adversely affect the quality of radio transmissions. In Algeria, it was primarily the presence of both the High and Middle Atlas Mountains, whereas in Vietnam, it was the vastness of jungle vegetation and the nearly constant high humidity levels that resulted in a near-dismal failure of SIGINT activity. In spite of the use of Agent Orange to clear the vegetation, and the incredible amount of high-level strategic bombing (amounting to more tonnage than dropped in the entire Second World War), the Vietnam War ended in a stalemate.

We'd had a nice flight out here, over Ifrane and the Middle Atlas Mountains and out to the Sahara on what was to be our final flight of this mission. Once again, we'd sat in our fabric bucket seats alongside the wall of our RD4 (we wondered why we didn't have nice, comfortable seats like any other passenger), and we'd endured the bumpy landing on the camel trails. The RD4 was one of the best aircrafts ever built. There were two large inflated tires for the desert, powerful twin engines, and plenty of room to move around. Great airship, as far as we were concerned.

About that time, Ski reminded me that a couple of weeks before, just after we had landed, about twenty Berbers on horseback had come out of the mountains, down to the plains, and out to the fringe of the Sahara. It had looked like they might be attempting to disrupt us in some manner, and our evaluator had gone up to the cockpit to speak with the pilot. In just a minute or two, we heard the pilot call the Convair B-58 Hustler, which by then was probably thirty thousand feet up somewhere, and advise them of the situation. Next thing we knew, in what seemed to be just a split second, we heard the B-58 going by us, about a thousand feet up, probably around six hundred miles per hour, right toward the Berbers. In no time, it seemed, the plane was over them; then it pulled up into a dramatic climb, kicked in the afterburners, and blew through the sound barrier with a terrific sonic boom as it accelerated upward in supersonic flight. *Wow!* We instantly heard the sonic boom, and our evaluator, who was watching the Berbers through his binoculars, said the horses had thrown most of their riders and were scattering in all directions. That was the last we saw of the Berbers!

To us, however, the most bizarre thing about the whole experience was when we got off the plane and started to set up our equipment under the wing of the RD4. We suddenly noticed scorpions (tails raised menacingly) all over the place. They were usually underground, coming out only at night to burrow under our sleeping bags. This time, however, there were so many scurrying about on the sand that we had to move our equipment out into the sun, farther down the camel trail, for the next few hours. Unnerving, to say the least. Could it have been the sonic boom of the B-58 only a short time before? We'll never know.

Back to the story. This trip was about to turn into something totally unexpected, to say the least, and one that would have a tremendous impact on our remaining time in Naval Intelligence and our life after the military.

Since we had arrived in North Africa, our assignment had been similar to that on Guam, monitoring Soviet submarines. But here, we were monitoring Soviet submarines in the Black Sea and the Mediterranean—until recently, when we were given this assignment out on the Sahara Desert: guerrilla communications intelligence. We were no longer chasing Soviet submarines; we were now on a special mission, locating, tracking, and intercepting OAS (Organisation de l'armée secrète) and FLN (Front de libération nationale, the National Liberation Front) guerrilla CW radio traffic in randomly targeted areas of Algeria.

It was one hell of a complex task—entirely different from locating, tracking, and intercepting organized military and government-supported groups as well as those opposed to the French government. Typical SIGINT communications between opposing forces in any war . . . same old, same old. Anyway, nothing we considered really valuable had happened since we started this TDA, much like the same mission on board the submarine on Guam. In fact, Ski and I had never heard our evaluator comment about our work; he'd just come up to us periodically, grab a stack of our work product, glance at it for a minute or two, and head back inside the aircraft. I'd search the frequencies, locate a transmitter target, and start copying. Ski would start a target triangulation location search, get a hit, and move on. Lots of routine in this job.

But this trip out to our location on the camel trail was different. What happened stunned us both. The evaluator picked up my stack of intercept work and suddenly gasped; he said something like, "Jesus, it's the French" or "the military" or something similar. Most of the radio transmission was in Arabic, but Ski verified that the physical location of the radio transmitter was actually on a French military base in Algeria. Our evaluator tore the messages I had just intercepted from my mill, told me to continue copying, and nearly sprinted back to the plane!

Five minutes passed. Still nothing. Another five minutes passed. Nothing. Ski and I looked at some of the material he hadn't taken back with him to the aircraft. The work was mostly in French or Arabic—non-encrypted, plain language text, which I couldn't read—with an occasional proper name thrown in for good measure: a city, or village, or person, I supposed. About then, he called us back to the aircraft, and ten minutes later we were on our way back to Sidi Slimane Air Base.

Little did we know at that moment that the material he had taken was indeed related to the military, except it was the

French military, not a guerrilla unit, and it involved a plot to assassinate General Charles de Gaulle. That must have been the reason we were out there on the desert in the first place. Probably someone in Washington had run across some evidence of such a plot against de Gaulle, had perhaps looked a little deeper, and eventually reached a decision to pursue the possibility and gather some intelligence. They were certainly aware of one thing: Unknown to most people, de Gaulle had, over the years, somehow survived over thirty assassination attempts.

And here's the rest of the story: We subsequently learned that a General Raoul Salan, a French military general serving as commander in chief of French forces in Algeria during the French-Algerian war, had been calling for the return to power of General de Gaulle, who he believed would protect a French Algeria rather than allow an independent Algeria. Unknown to many, he was also the founder and a principal member of the OAS, which was opposed to Algerian independence. Because of his actions to ensure that Algeria remained French, he was banned by the French government from entering Algeria in 1960, not long after we had uncovered his name in what we'd thought was a clandestine guerrilla radio transmission.

However, in spite of being banned from entering Algeria, he returned there in 1961, and in April 1962, he was arrested, charged with treason, and sentenced to death. The death sentence was commuted to life imprisonment, but he was pardoned in 1968. General Salan and Jean-Marie Bastien-Thiry, who was a colonel in the French Air Force, had been associates for many years in the early portion of the war. Like General Salan, Bastien-Thiry had been a Gaullist, but when he learned that de Gaulle had decided to grant Algeria its independence, a much-opposed move by many notable French military members and citizens, he contacted the OAS, where he apparently reestablished his relationship with General Salan, leading to the 1959 (and later 1962) assassination attempt of General de Gaulle, in which Ski and I had unknowingly been involved through our intercept activities under the wing of the RD4 in the Sahara Desert.

On August 22, 1962, Bastien-Thiry led the most prominent of several assassination attempts on de Gaulle's life in the Paris suburb of Petit-Clamart. Although de Gaulle's vehicle was hit numerous times by machine gun fire, de Gaulle and his wife and entourage escaped unharmed. The event was chronicled in detail in the 1971 historical novel *The Day of the Jackal* by Frederick Forsyth, and it was dramatized in the 1973 film adaptation of the same name. The OAS did exist as described in the novel, and the book opens with an accurate depiction of the attempt on de Gaulle's life, led by Jean-Marie Bastien-Thiry. But the account of the OAS hiring a British-born assassin in 1963 to kill Charles de Gaulle was pure fiction, and at the time, it was considered to be a spy thriller in poor taste, since General de Gaulle was still alive, having retired from public life in February 1970, when Forsyth sought a publisher. Charles de Gaulle passed away from natural causes at his country home in November 1970, and Forsyth eventually convinced a small U.K. publisher to print eight thousand copies of his book in June 1971. By 1975, over two and a half million copies were sold worldwide. In 1972 the book earned Forsyth the Edgar Allan Poe Award for Best Novel.

Jean-Marie Bastien-Thiry was arrested when he returned from a mission in the U.K., and he was brought to trial before a military tribunal that ran from January 28 to March 4, 1963. He was sentenced to death and executed by a firing squad on March 11, 1963. He was the last person to be executed by firing squad in France.

This was our last mission out to the Sahara Desert. We were back with the Soviet submarines, once again.

TEN

CHARLES DE GAULLE AND
THE FINAL FAREWELL

We hadn't been back to the desert for three or four weeks, although we were still on our monitoring mission via our equipment located in the operations building in the antenna field on our usual EVE-DAY-MID watch schedule. The mission was still foremost in our minds on every watch, but we'd not been told nor heard anything more.

It was probably around the fourth week after the intercept on the desert in February that Ski and I were awakened around 0300 after the EVE watch by one of the Marines on guard duty that night. He had two sets of Marine fatigues with him; he asked us to put them on and get our navy blue cap, and he told us that we were to report to the front gate ASAP. We didn't know what was going on. We got dressed, boots and all, and left for the front gate. A Navy jeep was there, along with our evaluator, who was dressed in his formal brown uniform, not his work clothing. We thought that was unusual, to say the least. Then, on our way to Sidi Slimane Air Base once again, we really wondered what was going on because neither of us had our code books or other material with us. When we arrived at Sidi Slimane, the guard at the gate just motioned us through, and we continued down the approach road, past some barracks, just like before, through the entrance gate to the runways, out and down to our aircraft at the end of the auxiliary runway—same as we had done several times before.

We drove past hangars and maintenance buildings, jet aircraft lined up on the extended runways, toward our aircraft, the RD4, idling and ready to go. Next thing I knew, we were seated in our fabric seats, running down the runway, and up into the night sky. I turned to Ski and said something like, "What the hell is this all about? There's always something they don't want you to know, but this is getting to be a pain in the ass." Ski replied, "Yeah, it's been like this ever since we got out of school and were sent to Guam." Our evaluator, in his fancy dress uniform, just stared at us.

About thirty minutes later, we heard the pilot talking to our cover, which we assumed was the B-58 Hustler, although this time we hadn't seen him on the runway. We were approaching the camel trails, then descending, taxiing for a minute or two—finally, engines off and a dead stop. Quiet. "Yeah. All quiet on the Western front," Ski said. No response.

Why was it so damn quiet? Why was there absolutely no noise at all? Just what was going on? I don't think even today it ever dawned on us just what was taking place. Why we were out there again, with no equipment, nothing but a set of fatigues. Nothing. Not a sound. Pilot speaking to our cover. *No, that's not our cover he is talking to. He's speaking French! Who in the hell is he talking to?* The co-pilot opened the cabin door. Our evaluator said, "Let's go, men. Stay beside me. Listen to my commands." *What the hell?* I'm thinking, and God only knows what Ski's thinking. Down the stairwell, around the wing, ahead toward a dim light roughly a quarter mile ahead of us.

After we were ordered to stop, the evaluator told us to march forward. Soon, three figures appeared directly ahead of us in the early morning mist. *Can't make anything out in the dim light. There appears to be an aircraft there, in back of the three figures. What is it?* I'm thinking. *Has a double tail. Never seen one like it before.* "Don't tell me we're getting on it," I wanted to yell. No, we weren't going to get on it—or even close to it. *Calm down, Minnick!* I told myself.

About halfway to the aircraft, we could see the three figures better. Appeared to be some type of military officers. One was taller than the other two—really tall. Ski was six feet four inches, and this guy appeared to be taller than that. Who were they? Why were we all out there in the desert? In the early, early morning, the sun wasn't up yet, although it wouldn't be long before it would be. I don't recall my exact emotions at that moment, but I think they were a combination of confusion, anxiety, curiosity, and excitement—and some that I can't recall. No fear, though, just *what the hell?*

Then we were face to face. Our evaluator said, "At ease," and then spoke to the three men in fluent French. He saluted the tallest man, who then extended his hand to our evaluator. They shook hands, and our evaluator extended handshakes to the other two men. He then said "Attention" to us—we, of course, complied—and then he said, "Hand salute," to which we also complied. Next our evaluator said—and here is where I nearly lost it—"Men, this is General Charles de Gaulle, of France." I'd known it, or thought I knew it, for maybe the last few minutes when I could clearly see the man. Neither Ski nor I had ever actually seen him before—maybe a picture or so over the preceding few years or in high school, but never this! I can't tell you what it felt like at that moment. Incredible. Unreal.

Our evaluator informed us that General de Gaulle had requested this meeting through our State Department after learning through the National Security Agency that the U.S. Navy had uncovered a potential assassination plot against General de Gaulle's life, and it involved certain French military officers. During his discussions with the State Department, he had learned of the Naval Security Group's involvement in uncovering the plot, and he wanted to thank those men personally for their part in exposing the plot to assassinate him.

General de Gaulle then extended his hand to Ski and me and said, "*Merci beaucoup.*" And then he said something in French that meant "a fine job you have done" and "good luck"—so we were told by our evaluator. General de Gaulle then exchanged some words with our evaluator, and the three of them turned and headed for their aircraft.

Our evaluator later told us that General de Gaulle had asked him to inform us that it was his practice to personally thank those individuals who had been instrumental in uncovering an assassination plot against his life and that this latest attempt was one of many such attempts over the years.

When we first had been accepted into Naval Intelligence back in 1955, and SIGINT directly, we were told we were the "hunters and gatherers" of the intelligence community. All Ski and I knew was that we'd been on a hunting trip and had gathered some prey. It had been a mighty important hunting trip, if we did say so.

On the afternoon of May 7, 1959, on the EVE watch, Ski and I received notification that Captain M. J. Smith, base commander, would be holding an awards ceremony at 0900 the next morning on the grounds of the admin building. When we asked if we were required to attend, since it would be during our DAY watch, we were told that, of course, we were required to be in attendance. So this meant we'd not have to go to the DAY watch. When we inquired, we were told that, of course, we would have to go to our DAY watch: "Why'd you think otherwise?" More about this later, but Ski and I never did get used to this EVE-DAY-MID watch routine. Why couldn't we just work Monday to Friday, 0900 to 1700? He told us we were required to wear our dress whites and that we'd better not be late.

The next morning, we got up with the rest of the guys on

our watch. They put on their blue work clothes while we put on our dress whites, and we headed out to the chow hall for breakfast. We knew something was up, but what it was we didn't have the slightest idea. At the chow hall, we got a lot of static from the guys, but we didn't know any more about the ceremony than they did. After the others left for the DAY watch, we hung around, drank some coffee, wandered out to the tennis courts, watched for a while, then headed over to base headquarters around 0830 and watched ship's company prepare for the ceremony.

All NSG personnel, except those on the DAY watch, were required to be in attendance, and soon roughly sixty-five men, all in dress whites, began appearing. We asked a chief who appeared to be in charge where we should be seated and were told port side of row two, up front. Okay, now we knew something was up, although I don't recall either of us discussing it. In our nearly four years of duty, neither of us had been to an awards ceremony, with the exception of the time we'd been promoted to CT3 on Guam and received our classification as NCOs. CT2, maybe, but why now? I was getting out in just over a month and had no plans to ship over (to reenlist). Ski and I had made plans to eventually attend Florida State University once we were discharged from active duty. So we had no idea what was going to take place. However, we'd see shortly.

Soon we saw Captain Smith up on the platform in front of the stands, along with two or three other officers we didn't know. The chief, who had been there earlier, put a record of the national anthem on the portable record player, tested the volume, and waited for the go-ahead from the captain. He soon got it and played the national anthem. Then the captain moved to the podium and said, "All be seated." He looked out at the audience and said something to the effect of "We're here this morning to present two commendation letters from the Chief of Naval Operations, Admiral Arleigh Burke, and the head of Naval Security Group, Captain James A. Morrison, U.S.N., one to Donald G. Lewandowski, CT3, and another to Robert W. Minnick Jr., CT3.

"All rise. Lewandowski and Minnick, please come forward." Once we got up on the platform, he said, "At ease. All please be seated. I have with me today a representative from headquarters, Naval Security Group, in Washington. He brings a letter of appreciation to this command, based on a memorandum from the Chief of Naval Operations, commending the Naval Security Group for its contributions to a special operation of prime importance and significance. It reads, 'The contribution of the Naval Security Group in support of this operation attests to the importance of the work it is doing and to the skill and devotion to duty of its personnel. . . . It is requested that you convey to those involved my heartiest congratulations and my appreciation for a job well done.' Signed Arleigh Burke, Admiral, U.S. Navy."

Captain Smith continued, "Along with the commendation from the Chief of Naval Operations and the personal 'Well Done' of the Naval Security Group, I wish to add my appreciation for your personal contribution and devotion to duty, which made this operation successful. This reflects great credit upon the Naval Security Group department of this command and is in keeping with the highest traditions of the Naval service."

Well, that was that, and we finally knew what the ceremony was all about. The next thing we heard was the playing of "Anchors Aweigh" and "Dis-*missed*." Ski and I then caught the first bus to the operations building for the remainder of our DAY watch.

Like everything else about the intelligence community, we never knew exactly what it was that resulted in this commendation. Nothing from anyone—not at that moment, not when I finished my enlistment and received my honorable discharge, not later, when I requested a copy of the commendation from the NSG. Nothing about what this great honor was all about. But in our hearts, we believe we knew what it was about. And why. And that's all that really mattered to both of us. The journey into the Sahara Desert was finally over. Back to the Black Sea and the Soviet submarines.

After the events of the day, Ski and I went back to the barracks, put on our shorts, got our tennis rackets, and went out to the courts. It was probably the best match we ever played, for some reason, but neither of us let up for perhaps an hour or so, and I don't even remember who won or what the score was. I've often thought about that day—one of the great moments of my life, and Ski felt the same. It leads me to this.

Both of us were nearing the end of our four-year tour of duty and would soon be heading back to the States for discharge. Me in July and Ski in August. What then? Reenlist for another tour? No assurance that we'd stay together. Where? In Winter Harbor, Maine, or Washington, D.C.? Maybe back to California? After two consecutive overseas tours, we'd get our pick. Try for Officer Candidate School? Or get out of the Navy and go to work for the National Security Agency in Washington? Neither of us had ever really given much thought to this aspect of our tour—since Imperial Beach in 1956—to how it would end. And there were no guarantees. But then, what guarantees are there in life?

We'd grown very close. We had a great deal in common: played sports together, gone on leave and liberty together, drank too much beer and gotten into too many fights over the years—not with each other, but as "brothers." Sounds simplistic, but maybe that was really what it was. We were like brothers. And we'd accomplished some remarkable things during our career, ending with this awards ceremony. Something we did really mattered. And it mattered to a lot of people. And that was, for some reason, very important to both of us. Extraordinarily important to both of us.

Later that day, Ski asked me if I still intended to go to FSU.

We hadn't talked about that for a long time. I couldn't even remember the last time. Maybe it was on Guam. We'd both had great times there and, since I was from Florida, Ski had always joked about checking it out to see if everything I had told him about Florida was true. It surprised me that he'd ask, because that was the answer for both of us. Recently, I'd been thinking about maybe trying for OCS or going to work at NSA. But I still had an uneasy feeling about my future. When Ski asked me about FSU, all my thoughts and concerns—and, yeah, worries, I guess—about the end of my tour in the Navy sort of melted away.

I said to him, "Yeah, Ski, I'm still thinking about going. How about you?"

"Yeah, yeah, I'd like to do that."

"Really? Let's go to town and celebrate. We don't have much time left."

That's when we knew what our future held in store for us.

I finished my four-year enlistment in July 1959. I was at the Naval station in Norfolk, Virginia, after a long flight from Casablanca to the Azores, Newfoundland, and Virginia. We went over my records and other routine matters, future benefits, medical status, etc. During my Naval Security Group security debriefing, the separation officer asked if I wanted to reenlist. I told him no. He suggested I could sign up for an additional six years and attend OCS. He explained the benefit and why I qualified, including that it could lead to a career with the National Security Agency when I did get out of the Navy. Again, I said no thanks, that my buddy and I planned to go to college. He opened his drawer, pulled out a form-type letter, gave it to his assistant, told him to prepare it for his signature, turned to me, and said something to the effect of "When you're ready to go to college, send this letter to the registrar. It's all you'll need. No high school records, no test scores, no references—just this letter. You shouldn't have any problems. If you do, let us know. Good luck to you, sailor."

That was just about all there was to that. I thanked him, picked up my separation papers and the letter, and got a ride to the front gate of the station for a cab to the airport. I remember thinking, just briefly, that at that very moment, I'd rather be back in Africa with my buddies. No, I quickly dismissed that and got in the cab. I flew into Miami International, where Mom and my stepfather picked me up, and an hour later, we were home in Pompano Beach.

The next day I called Jacksonville University, asked them to mail me an application, and headed to the nearest Ford dealer, where I bought a 1952 Ford two-door coupe for about $200. I got my temporary tag and headed out to Fort Lauderdale and the beach!

Not bad. With my mustering-out pay and savings, I still had a chunk of change. I had chosen Jacksonville University, a small, four-year, liberal-arts college in Jacksonville, Florida, after reading about it in the base library in Sidi Yahia before I left Africa. I thought it might give me a head start on Ski's and my plan to go to Florida State University in the near future. Ski wouldn't get his discharge until late August, and he had decided to stick around Pittsburgh for the next year, to get up enough money to pay out-of-state tuition. Unlike wartime vets, Ski and I didn't get G.I. education benefits at the present time, so we knew we'd be working on and off campus sometime soon. Both Ski and I had an advantage: The only leave we'd taken was 15 days after boot camp, another 15 days after radio school, 30 days after our tour on Guam (plus a week in Africa)—while we had earned 30 days annually during our enlistment, a total of 120 days paid leave. Back in those times, that was a chunk of money.

I got my acceptance to JU in a few weeks (I saved the Navy letter for FSU), and by September 1, I was in Jacksonville, had a part-time job on campus, and was ready for school to start. Ski told me he'd found a job in Pittsburgh and hoped to start school at FSU the following fall. He'd also gotten one of those special Navy letters, which we rightly or wrongfully felt were somehow related to the commendations we'd received in Africa.

I was enrolled at JU for my freshman year, did well, and earned fifteen credit hours toward my baccalaureate degree that year. I'd laid the foundation, and now it was time to get back to Pompano Beach, where I lived with Mom and my stepdad from June 1960 to July 1962. As soon as I got back from Jacksonville, I took a job as a stock clerk on the receiving dock of the newly constructed Jordan Marsh department store, located on Atlantic Boulevard near the Intracoastal Waterway, about three blocks from the Atlantic Ocean. It was a great job for a young guy out of the military, and my military service got me twenty-five cents an hour more than others. Another benefit was that my DD214 (active-duty discharge papers) got me an immediate job, starting the next morning, not the following week, as was the case with other staff workers (who were often required to undergo background checks). What was hardest for me was the fact that this job absolutely and completely failed to compare to the Navy job, and it took me a long, long time to appreciate that fact.

Good money in my pocket (forty hours at $1.25 an hour), no rent to pay, and every Friday night a jazz party after work at the Kasbah. This was an African-decor bar across the street from Jordan Marsh, where at least a fifth of the staff gathered daily after work to drink, dance, and listen to jazz. Great place. It reminded me of Africa, and much more. Hated to leave that place at 0100, and believe it or not, I never got into a fight! My days were to arrive at work at 0800, work to 1700, take off for the beach and dinner with a buddy or a girlfriend, then head for the Kasbah around 2100 to 0100, go home, sleep till 0700, five days a week. Good life. Best times were when colleges and universities let out for spring break, and twenty-five thousand or more students headed for Fort Lauderdale and the beaches. Those were extraordinary times, believe me! Spent many a night right on the beach. And it lasted roughly sixty days, usually all of April and May.

My life revolved around the Kasbah during those times I worked to save up for FSU. It was like a Kasbah in North Africa, and I even gave them a couple of sets of napkins and place mats I had brought back from Africa, together with some enlargements of photos of camels and Berbers from Casablanca and Meknes. In turn, I usually had a great reserved seat up front near the musicians.

ELEVEN

THE CUBAN MISSILE CRISIS

It is generally accepted that no single event in the history of the Cold War—and, indeed, of mankind—presented as great a challenge to world peace and the continued existence of humankind as the thirteen days of the Cuban Missile Crisis in October 1962.

On October 14, 1962, a U-2 spy plane, on a Strategic Air Command mission over Cuba, took a series of photographs that became the first direct evidence of Soviet medium-range ballistic missiles in Cuba. On the morning of October 16, National Security Advisor McGeorge Bundy presented a detailed analysis of the photographic evidence to President John Kennedy at an Oval Office briefing. Then President Kennedy convened a meeting of fourteen administration officials and advisers. The group became known as the Executive Committee of the National Security Council, otherwise known as EXCOMM.

The world was confronted by the extreme possibility of "Armageddon": the "final war between Good and Evil at the end of the world."

EXCOMM members soon received estimates from the Defense Department and intelligence services that the Soviet missiles could be fully operational within fourteen days, with individual missiles readied within eighteen hours. Most missiles were determined to be SS-4s (R-12s), with a range of approximately 1,265 statute miles. This placed major U.S. cities, including Dallas, Texas, and Washington, D.C., within a strike area. Later photographic evidence concluded that several SS-5s (R-14s) also existed, with a range of approximately 2,500 miles, placing Boston, Detroit, and Chicago within strike range.

For the next seven days, EXCOMM debated the merits of three general approaches to the developing crisis. The first was an air strike targeting as many missile sites as possible. The second was an air strike followed by a U.S. military invasion of Cuba. The third suggestion, by President Kennedy, was a blockade of Soviet ships presently en route to Cuba, which were believed to be carrying additional materials in support of the offensive weapons program.

While the U.S. had concentrated its efforts on aircraft and ICBMs after World War II, the USSR had been concentrating on submarine-launched ballistic missiles (SLBMs) and increasing its stockpile of both conventional and nuclear-powered submarines equipped with SLBMs as primarily an offensive weapon of war and secondarily as a defensive weapon. The U.S., on the other hand, was primarily focused on offensive long-range strategic aircraft equipped with nuclear missiles. While Germany had developed the V-2 ballistic missile variant, which could be launched by a submarine, when the war ended in 1945, German engineers and scientists who had worked on and developed the V-2 went to work for either the U.S. or the USSR on their specific ICBMs and SLBMs, respectively. Initially, the early SLBM systems required submarines to be surfaced when they fired ballistic missiles, but launch systems eventually were adapted, first by the USSR, to permit underwater launching in the 1950s and 1960s.

The USSR had launched the world's first SLBM, an R-11FM,

on September 16, 1955. Five more Soviet submarines became the world's first operational ballistic-missile submarines (SSBNs) with two R-11FM missiles each, which entered service in 1956 and 1957. The U.S. had introduced its first fully operational SSBN, the USS *George Washington*, in December 1959, and in July 1960 it had also conducted the first successful submerged SLBM launch with a Polaris A-1 ballistic missile. Roughly forty days later, the USSR had made its first successful underwater launch of a submarine ballistic missile in the White Sea. However, that project had been plagued with problems from the start, and submerged launches were not an operational capability for the USSR until October 1961, when it was able to beat the U.S. in launching and testing the first SLBM with a live nuclear warhead, an R-13. It's important to note that the dates just referred to were to play a critical role in the Cuban Missile Crisis in October 1962.

The short range of the early SLBMs of both the USSR and the U.S. dictated the berthing and deployment locations utilized by both countries. In addition, the full deployment of nuclear-powered, multiple-carrying ballistic submarines for both the USSR and the U.S. was not achieved until the late 1960s. The same holds true for Soviet and U.S. submarines carrying missiles with a range of 2,500 miles or greater and equipped with three or more nuclear warheads that detonated in a pattern around a single target. U.S. submarines were initially deployed at sites in Scotland, in Spain (Rota), and in Guam by the middle 1960s. The USSR's submarines were initially deployed in the Murmansk area for the Atlantic and the Vladivostok area for the Pacific, which required the USSR's submarines to make a long transit through the Atlantic or Pacific in order to adequately patrol the continental U.S. Unknown to the U.S. in the late 1950s and early 1960s, the USSR had undertaken the development of nuclear-powered SLBMs with nuclear warheads, as well as boats that were capable of launching newly developed ballistic missiles with

a greatly enhanced range (4,500 miles) and multiple inde-
pendently targeted reentry vehicles (MIRVs), which had
multiple nuclear warheads that could each hit a different
target.

Also unknown to the U.S., these submarines had been
built in a secret submarine base in Balaklava and berthed in
Odessa and Sevastopol in the Black Sea sometime between
the late 1950s and the early 1960s. This location required that
for the submarines to enter the Atlantic, they would have to
pass through the Strait of Bosporus, the Sea of Marmara, the
Dardanelles, the Aegean Sea and into the Mediterranean, and
then through the Strait of Gibraltar and into the Atlantic. On
this journey, there would be numerous opportunities to detect
their location from NSG sites in the Mediterranean, the Strait
of Gibraltar, Morocco, Spain, and the Azores. These facts also
played a significant role in the Cuban Missile Crisis.

Throughout the duration of the Cold War, ballistic-missile
submarines were of great strategic importance for the U.S.
and the USSR. The primary reason for this is that of all the
weapons of war since time began, only the submarine can
hide from reconnaissance aircraft and ships and can launch
nuclear weapons from beneath the sea with virtual impunity.
This makes submarines nearly immune to a first-strike direct
attack against nuclear forces, allowing each opponent to
maintain the capability to launch a devastating retaliatory
strike, even if all land-based missiles have been destroyed.
Furthermore, the deployment of highly accurate nuclear missiles on ultra-quiet submarines allows an attacker to sneak up
close to an enemy coast and launch a missile on a depressed
trajectory, thus opening the possibility of a decapitation strike.

It was cold. My white wool Navy blanket was bundled up on
the floor, and I was freezing my ass off. It had turned cold the
night before, and we'd all come in from drinking beer on the

front porch of the house. This was Florida in the early fall, and we were in a boarding house with no heat. If you wanted heat, you had to buy yourself a room heater. The same held true for the summer months: You purchased a small room fan because summers could be scorching in Tallahassee (some fifty miles from the Gulf of Mexico and its great beaches). I should have thought about the weather and not finished off that last six-pack of Red Stripe. Now I was paying the price.

The autumn days of September and October were generally pleasant there in Tallahassee, even with some color in the changing leaves, unlike in Fort Lauderdale, which was still a near constant eighty-five and sixty-five degrees, day and night. I also knew that the temperatures would change shortly, just in time for some great nighttime football games and parties. But the short days of winter there might be rough, especially if you lived in an old, poorly insulated three-bedroom shack that had been converted into a five-and-a-half-bedroom home of sorts at 403 West College Avenue, just off the campus of FSU. It was across the street from where my Navy buddy, Don Lewandowski, had a room a hell of a lot bigger and better than mine. Well, shit, I reached down, grabbed my blanket, pulled it up over myself, and tried to doze off.

"Bob, get your ass up!" Ski yelled through the door. "We're going to get breakfast at the Sweet Shop."

"What time is it?" I asked.

"It's seven-thirty," Ski muttered. "Come on, get your ass up."

I knew I'd done right scheduling my first class after 0900. So I got up, put on my jeans and T-shirt, and grabbed my favorite Jordan Marsh Madras shirt and my jacket—yeah, the one from Africa, the one we'd worn the week before, when we went to dinner at the Sweet Shop and had a confrontation with some FSU football players. Great start to the fall semester *that* had turned out to be. That's how the twenty-second day of October 1962 had started. Roughly twelve hours later, we would be completely enmeshed in the news—President Kennedy's nationwide announcement regarding what soon became the Cuban Missile Crisis.

I had had a feeling of foreboding on October 16 after calling my stepfather in Pompano Beach. He had left a message for me at the Tallahassee boarding house. When we spoke, he told me Mom had received a call from someone with the Navy in Washington who wanted to speak with me. I was surprised, mainly because I hadn't heard from the Navy since my discharge from active duty in July 1959. I was, however, still under obligation as an inactive reserve member until July 1963.

Ski and I first learned about the Cuban Missile Crisis the day President Kennedy made his announcement on TV (October 22, 1962). The whole school was talking, and then there was that phone call from the Navy in Washington.[12] We didn't find out the reason for the call until President Kennedy held his nationwide televised address regarding the situation. Ski and I had talked about the call on the sixteenth, but we really didn't get too concerned about it until President Kennedy's TV address. Talk was all over the university campus—students, professors, the administration, classrooms, cafeteria, fraternities, even the ROTC units were really concerned. The issues ranged from whether to cancel scheduled football games and other athletic events, grant employees emergency leave—on and on it went. Each day seemed like it got more and more hysterical as the week progressed.

Once we heard the president's remarks, however, our concern became real. We looked at the events differently, with a critical, informed view from our military experience and from our historical perspective of what we knew from our tour,

---

12. The reason for this phone call remains a mystery. BJ passed away before his collaborator, cousin Lindy, could ask him. Chapter 11 had not been written, and Lindy had to craft it with what she was given.

both on Guam and in North Africa. We just knew that the Navy was involved in the crisis. But from the beginning of the crisis, and after listening to the president, we both felt that something was missing—something absolutely critical and as astounding as anything we had become aware of in the performance of our intelligence duties.

Why was there no discussion of a solution? As the week went on, with more and more presidential comments and discussions, we both came to the conclusion that this couldn't be the real situation. Threats of outright war? Discussion about impeachment of the president if we didn't take military action against Cuba—or even against the USSR? An embargo to stop the movement of more nuclear missiles into Cuba? Thousands of U.S. Marines moving to south Florida for a planned military invasion of Cuba? Strategic Air Command aircraft, armed with nuclear missiles and other weapons, activated and flying in and out of military and commercial airports around the world—and as one lands, another takes off?

Our first discussion, as I remember it, was "What is the real story here?" Then: "Jesus, the U.S. better get its act together, before it is too late." Did we think we knew what really was going on here? Yes, we did. And it turns out, we were right.

Ski and I spent time on a computer at the Catholic Student Center, and later we stopped by the university library to do some more looking. First of all, we both knew that if anything were really happening, it originated in the Black Sea (Odessa) and probably involved the USSR's rapidly developing nuclear submarine fleet. We had spent the past seventeen months in North Africa working that situation, much the same as on Guam. That was one of the reasons we'd been sent to North Africa in the first place: our experience with Soviet submarine communications.

What we immediately knew was that if the USSR had sent a flotilla of forty-some ships to Cuba, many with the storage of missile-launching silos in open sight on the decks, they were up to something extraordinary—more than met the eye. Then when we observed U-2 photos of missile silos already erected on Cuban soil, we both immediately knew they were a ruse, purposefully designed to "alert" us to their intentions (which had nothing to do at all with the flotilla and the already-erected missile silos). Most important, the missile silos were for short-range missiles, and that didn't make any sense. To us, they were simply for show purposes—especially the one photo that showed a Soviet officer taking a leak next to one of the silos (this photo later hung on the wall in Kennedy's office). To us, at this point, it all looked like a high school game being played by kids.

This wasn't a power play by the USSR, even though both Cuba and the USSR were still pissed off about the CIA's "Bay of Pigs" failed invasion, etc., and they weren't conducting exercises for fun either. This was for real. But what was it that was for real? Was the USSR really planning to stop what they thought were recent attempts by the U.S. to undertake an invasion of Cuba? If so, why all the short-range missile silos? To threaten Miami? That was a joke. And if the USSR actually thought we were planning an invasion of Cuba, what proof did they have?

Cuba was then, and has been ever since the Castro revolution, nothing more than a small, insignificant Communist blip in our hemisphere and barely a part of the Cold War. Yet here we were. Maybe Khrushchev was just playing a power game. If so, we didn't appear to be—at the beginning—very much concerned. We also knew that since *Sputnik* had been launched in 1957, the Navy had been aggressively working to ensure the security of the oceans throughout the world. The USSR, unlike the U.S., had concentrated its offensive war capabilities since the end of World War II on surface and underwater capabilities, including nuclear missile development and nuclear-powered submarines as its primary offensive weapons, while the U.S. was focused on the Strategic Air Command.

Associated with the Kennedy announcement of a blockade was the fact that a single diesel submarine was being aggressively pursued by Navy ships and aircraft at the time of the initial crisis.

Ski and I knew virtually everything there was to know about Soviet submarine communications and capability. How many they had—class, weapons, where they were built, where their bases were located—everything. As SIGINT operatives, we were especially concerned about their communications. And we had an ace in the hole. Thanks to what appeared to be a new form of communications, based on World War II German intelligence and named *Kurier*, they had inadvertently disclosed it to us when they'd launched *Sputnik*. In their rush to be first in space back in 1957, the USSR had given away all there was to know about their greatest offensive weapon—the submarine.

At first, we'd been at a loss as to how to decrypt it. But shortly thereafter, NSA and NSG had determined what their new communication was—how to detect it, how to intercept it, how to decode its encrypted messages, and how to pinpoint the location of the submarine—whether on the sea or beneath it. We could track it and project its course from roughly 3,500 miles from our land-based intelligence stations.

We also learned during the next few days that since July 1962, the U.S. military had been planning coordinated Air Force and Navy air strikes over Cuba by September, while at the same time the Kennedy administration had started developing plans for a Naval blockade—plans to inspect each Soviet trawler headed for Cuba. If missile silos or any nuclear weapons were found, the trawler would be denied further passage to Cuba.

We knew, from our previous intelligence work, that the Navy had been implementing updated intelligence capability of a defensive nature within the framework of its existing Atlantic and Pacific HF/DF networks. ECHELON, SOSUS, and BULLSEYE projects were included because they complemented what had been in place since the *Sputnik* launch in 1957.

Although there was no formal mention of it, it was clear to us that Kennedy knew of the actions of the USSR over the past months, about moving short-range missiles and missile silos into Cuba, as well as the fact that the USSR's ultimate plans certainly included building submarine pens on the island at some point. It was no secret that the USSR, ever since the start of the Cold War, was intent on developing a nuclear-powered and nuclear-equipped guided-missile submarine fleet, capable of delivering a full-fledged nuclear attack anywhere in the world.

It had all started with the construction of a submarine base at a top-secret military facility located at Balaklava in the Ukraine on the Black Sea. That site, which Ski and I were familiar with since our tour in North Africa in 1958–1959, was located underground at Mount Tavros; it included numerous submarine pens, dry dock and repair facilities, and weapons storage areas, and it could house scientists and engineers, submarine crew members, and others, while protecting them from nuclear fallout or a direct hit by a nuclear bomb. Entrance to and from the site to the open sea was through a tunnel protected with extensive camouflage devices and equipment. The principal tunnel was approximately a quarter of a mile long and could house up to roughly fifteen submarines. There was also a storage area for nuclear weapons. Constructions of the Balaklava submarine pens had started shortly after *Sputnik* was launched in 1957, about the time Ski and I were transferred to North Africa. It was completed around 1960.

The USSR had only a few nuclear-powered and -equipped submarines, all built at Balaklava on the Black Sea. By the time the USSR attempted to develop missile launchers and nuclear-equipped submarines in Cuba in 1962, the U.S. Navy, with the aid of SOSUS, was able to track each and every one of them—and was able to progress further ahead of the USSR in the production of nuclear-powered and -equipped submarines.

Looking back on the early years of the Cold War, and on the Cuban Missile Crisis in particular—and with the benefit of hindsight and hands-on experience—it was clear to Ski and to me that SIGINT, combined with other types of intelligence, had initially pinpointed Cuba (in concert with the USSR) as a grave and lethal threat to the U.S. and, as it turns out, the entire world. War was no longer simply a conflict between two nations but had become a lethal threat to the survival of the entire human race.

The massive offensive and defensive arms buildup since the end of World War II had focused the president and military leaders of the U.S. on the threat from Cuba and the USSR long before the crisis erupted. Toward the end, the intelligence community, together with SOSUS, gave President Kennedy the information he needed to extricate the nation from its most dire crisis since the end of World War II.

TWELVE

FINAL THOUGHTS

I t was a long journey.

On the one hand, many of us think of life as a long, challenging, and enduring journey into some type of glory and peace in our later years. But if you've fought the battle in your youthful days, what is there to even compare?

On the other hand, maybe all of those youthful days were of no importance. Maybe all that really matters, if the youthful days were challenging enough, is that it was enough, back then, just to have done it—to have been there in the early days of the Cold War in the Pacific Islands, virtually in the Black Sea, and in North Africa, and finally to have come face to face with Armageddon during the Cuban Missile Crisis in the Atlantic Ocean and the Caribbean Sea.

Others like us will do it again, sometime, but not in those places and in that way. Those times are gone, and the events have vanished. They were dangerous events of the times, with their own extraordinary challenges and unique technology. And they were faced by two brothers who gave of themselves unselfishly and became the first line of defense—the hunters and gatherers of the intelligence community.

In the end, if you've done a good job and somebody

knows and appreciates it, that's about as good as life gets, whether it was earlier or later in life.

This has been the story of U.S. Navy SIGINT from *Sputnik* to the Cuban Missile Crisis, and how the buildup of SOSUS saved mankind from extinction. It wasn't President Kennedy's negotiating skills, nor was it something that happened in secret EXCOMM meetings in the Oval Office. A Naval courier, on his way to a personal meeting with Khrushchev, carried a black box containing images that documented the exact physical location of the USSR's entire fleet of submarines everywhere in the world—from Odessa in the Black Sea, to Vladivostok in the western Pacific, to Murmansk, and under the Atlantic and Arctic Oceans. Approximately ten hours later, Khrushchev and Kennedy announced a resolution to the crisis, wherein the U.S. agreed to withdraw U.S. missiles from Turkey, while in return the USSR agreed to withdraw its nuclear missiles and other war materials from Cuba.

The Navy had created such a fortress with its globally linked underwater Sound Surveillance System (SOSUS) that a Soviet submarine knew it would be detected wherever it was in the ocean—only to be threatened with being blown to bits by ASW if it surfaced. The USSR respected the quarantine not because we withdrew missiles and troops from Turkey but because we "had them cornered" with SOSUS, and they knew it.

The U.S. Navy and Naval Intelligence had, in the end, provided the president with all the information needed to extricate the U.S. from its most dire crisis since the end of World War II. We had avoided Armageddon.

May your life's journey be one of pride and joy. And may it always be with "Fair Winds and Following Seas."

Robert W. Minnick Jr., CT3, U.S. Navy (deceased)
Donald G. Lewandowski, CT3, U.S. Navy (deceased)

[A postscript to this comes in the form of an excerpt from one of BJ's letters to Lindy, dated March 22, 2017.]

You know something? In attempting to write my story, I've had occasions to really, really look back, think about, and remember my past. I've woken up in the middle of the night on numerous occasions, grabbed a pen or pencil, and started writing down my thoughts. I'm eternally grateful for this opportunity to recall and re-live my life. It has changed me in too many ways to discuss here. My sincere and deepest appreciation and love for this opportunity, and you.

P. S. Since I started, nearly a year ago, I've had a desire to write a song about my life. It's nearly finished now, and Mimi's daughter Kelly is—hopefully—composing the music: guitar, piano, harmonica, and drums (all family instruments at one time or another that had a profound impact on me over the years).

Love,

Robert Wood Minnick Jr.

BJ'S SONG

He sailed out to sea, looking for answers
To questions that bothered him so.
He was aggressive, young, and impressive,
Seeking the world on his own,
But the warm tropical breezes
And swaying palm trees,
The girls, and the beaches
Put his ambitions at bay.

And warm summers and cold winters
And beaches and deserts
Crossed paths like sprinters,
And four years passed quickly away.

And soon he was home and off to college
And married a girl named Mary.
They had a fine life; she was a good wife
And bore him a fine daughter one day,
And soon a fine son along the way.
So, all of the answers to all of his questions
He locked in his attic one day
'Cause he cherished his life
And was a fine banker,
And thirty years passed quietly away.

But they soon took his job and comfortable life
And left him alone with all of his strife.
While the tears were falling, he was recalling
The answers he had long ago found.
So he hopped on a sailboat and sailed out to sea
And left his home without a sound.

Now he lives in the Islands, fishes the pilings,
And drinks his Red Stripe each day.
He's writing his memoirs and living alone,
And he doesn't care what people say.
But if he likes you, he'll smile and he'll say,
"Hey, some of it was magic, some of it tragic,
But I had a good life all the way."

And he sailed out to sea, looking for answers
to questions that bothered him so.

Robert Minnick Jr.
August 18, 2017

EPILOGUE

Featuring a blog entry by BJ's daughter, Mimi

Robert Wood Minnick Jr. (BJ) passed away at his home in Blountstown, Florida, on June 18, 2018. Surviving him are his brother, Bruce; daughter, Mimi; and son, John Minnick— as well as many grandchildren, nieces, and nephews. Four months later, Hurricane Michael made landfall in the Florida panhandle as a cat 5 storm. This was where BJ had lived for many years, enjoying his Red Stripe beer on the sandy beach-front in Port St. Joe,[13] where his daughter, Mimi, and granddaughter Kelly lived. He once told me that after a big storm, he liked to grab his folding chair and a six-pack of Red Stripe and sit on the beach, waiting for silver and gold coins to wash up from all the shipwrecks in the Gulf. But, alas, they never did.

Mimi wrote in her "Water Signs" blog that she and Kelly weathered the hurricane in Cloud Nine Cottage, which had become an island that day. This is an excerpt from the blog:

> Houses along Indian Pass Road and on the lagoon weren't so lucky, taking on eight feet or more of water. Back at my place, a

---

13. BJ lived in Port St. Joe for many years before moving to Blountstown.

mile down the road and closer to the beach, my neighbors along Apalachee, on an almost imperceptible rise of another old dune, took two and a half feet of water. These houses were older and low-built, not the stilt-built houses, which came later, closer to the ocean. Behind me, on Palm Street, houses took from two to four feet of water. It took weeks to clean them up. Some had to be demolished.

I rolled the downed telephone pole blocking the door to one side. It had literally acted as a battering ram, pushing the frame of the porch door back several inches, which made it difficult to open. I didn't see the crack in the porch roof until much later. Thank God it didn't come further, it would have split the house in two like a plastic Easter egg.

There was a tiny pool of water at the front door, no more than what comes under the door in any blowing rain. And that was it. *Inside the house, it was as if there had been no hurricane at all.* Not a picture askew. Not a drop of water. No damage to the roof. I stood stock-still in the living room; the cottage is so tiny you can see all of it from the door. I thought I must be dreaming. I closed my eyes. Breathe in, breathe out. Opened my eyes again. I was not dreaming. My house had been spared.

I think I can never leave her now. Here, in this ramshackle little cottage we call Sunshine Daydream, I might be safe.

I went back out on the porch and called for my daughter. "It's fine! There's no water!" She looked at me like I was crazy, like maybe I'd really, finally lost my mind. I had, of course, but that had happened yesterday, watching the Gulf engulf us.

I started putting things back in their places, then unloaded my few treasures from the car, including my father's Navy jacket and an unpublished manuscript of his career in Naval Intelligence, the final chapter still unfinished the day before he was found lifeless on the floor just four months before the storm. The death certificate read "sudden death," but I know he died of a broken heart. My mother had died just four months earlier than him. They'd been together since she was nineteen years old, and to her dying day, he loved her with the same passion he felt the first time he'd laid eyes on her. She'd put us all through hell by refusing treatment for bipolar disorder, which had afflicted her most of her life and all of mine. She'd burned many bridges, including the one that led to my heart. But never with my father, who remained faithful and true to her to the end. That's love. I lost them both in the span of four months. I'd already endured a hurricane of heartache. And now this.

He'd survived fifty-four years with her and was anxious to continue caring for her in the afterlife. But he survived another four months without her, so he could finish the book, full of adventure and Cold War intrigue. Astonishing tales of intercepting signals from *Sputnik*, the world's first satellite. Terrifying tales from a submarine taking on water deep in the Mariana Trench. Heroic stories of intercepting an assassination attempt on Charles de Gaulle and of meeting the beleaguered French president on a remote camel trail in the Sahara Desert. He'd written his story. Now he needed to take care of my mother in heaven, like he'd done for fifty-four years, come hell or high water. This angel had flown. Away from me.

His spirit lingered here, though, along with the last of his belongings and the unbroken remains of my deep love for him. He loved my little beach house because he loved the beach more than anything besides my mother. He told me often that when he died, I'd see him in the laughing gulls, swooping and diving along the shore. He was right. I see him almost every day.

Once, a few days after the storm, I'd gone to the ocean to bathe. We still had no water or electricity. Like Gilligan's Island. No phones, no lights, no motorcars, not a single luxury. Well, we did have phones, but the cell towers had been destroyed. And we had motorcars; we just had no gas. All five gas stations on the coastal highway from Mexico Beach to Port St. Joe had been leveled. Only one has reopened, three months later.

After I bathed, I lay down in the sun. I must have drifted off. When I awoke, I felt some presence. Turning my head slightly, he was there. My father, in the form of a laughing gull. He stayed there for a long time, never laughing, just standing beside me, facing into the wind, as is their habit. I listened closely, but I couldn't hear what he was trying to say—perhaps only "I am here."

I spent many hours during those days sitting on my porch, pondering the devastation. The porch was the only place I felt safe emotionally. Dad liked the porch too; it was his favorite spot. He'd sit in the old yellow rocking chair, listening to the crashing surf and the breeze in the palms.

Sometimes he'd doze off there, an old man lost in dreams of North Africa and the Pacific Islands. I know this because invariably he'd wake up from one of these reveries with a story of glory days long past. I always listened, though I'd heard it all before. It was something in the way he came alive in the telling. I thought sometimes that the only thing keeping him alive was memory. It pulsed in his veins.

I see him now in the form of an angel standing on the porch of my cottage while the storm raged around my only refuge. I envision him young and strong, as in his Navy days. He has one hand uplifted, like Moses parting the waters. Facing into the wind. He had a mean left hook, and I see him deliver the blow to that bastard Michael at my doorstep. "Don't even think about it, buddy."

In truth, it was probably the chain-link fence that saved the house. I hated that ugly fence, but I love it now. Debris built up against it, forming a berm around three sides of the house. The water flowed around it until the fence came down with the telephone pole. Then that debris field piled up against the house, forming another dam. By then the waters must have been receding; otherwise, they would have flowed right over it and through the house.

There was an African American man in line in front of me at the dollar store two or three weeks after the storm. He was buying what looked like picnic supplies. The line was long, so we struck up a conversation. As is standard around here now, his first question was "Did you do okay?"

"By the grace of God," I replied.

He was a godly man, working here on relief efforts. He was buying huge quantities of chicken, ribs, and potato salad to feed a large crew of workers. He smiled, and I told him about my father parting the waters. Then I told him how it was really the fence.

"Why would you do that?" he asked.

"Do what?" I replied.

He looked into my eyes for a moment before speaking. "Who do you think held the fence?"

I smiled back. "You're right," I said. "It was my father, who art in heaven." He smiled and nodded. I looked into his eyes, and the spirit moved me to speak again. "And here you are, feeding the multitude."

He looked like he might cry. "Thank you," he said. "You have inspired me today."

MIMI MINNICK
Port St. Joe, Florida

EDITOR'S NOTE

Lindy Minnick

My cousin BJ had a special place in my heart too. My first memory of getting to know him was when he stopped by his uncle John's home in Arlington, Virginia, right before he shipped out on his Navy adventures to North Africa in 1958. I was fourteen, and I was captivated by his good looks, emerald green eyes, and infectious enthusiasm for life. His broad smile and easy laugh were Minnick traits I was very familiar with. He paid us one more visit after returning from North Africa, and he presented me with a gift of Shalimar perfume from Morocco. I still wear that delicious vanilla scent to this day.

APPENDIX

A Note About My Navy "Brother"

I first met Don Lewandowski ("Ski") at the Naval Training Center San Diego radio school in October 1955 after graduating from boot camp in Illinois. Those eight weeks were literal hell for all twenty-five of us, as we attempted to learn to type, take, and transmit CW Morse code in anticipation of qualifying for the Imperial Beach, California, spy school on the "Silver Strand."

All class members were just out of boot camp, undergoing National Security Agency security background checks for a top-secret clearance. As I recall, only one or two of the students at the radio school were transferred out in the first few weeks for "security" reasons rather than for failure to progress in the program.

At this time, Ski and I were merely students, as we were not yet paired as "brothers" on missions. Once we got our assignments at the conclusion of our Imperial Beach spy training, we would finalize our relationship at our first duty station in Guam. I was an HF/DF equipment operator, while Ski was a CW Morse code intercept operative. Working together, we would detect and locate the physical positioning of the radio-transmitting station that we had targeted for intercept purposes. We would stay together for the full term of our enlistment.

The following is Ski's obituary at www.legacy.com and featured in the Florida Times-Union:

LEWANDOWSKI, Donald G. Lewandowski, 73, passed away peacefully on January 15, 2010, surrounded by his loving family. He was a dedicated husband, father, grandpa, and friend who touched the lives of countless people with his selflessness and love of life.

His sense of humor, gentle spirit, and strength inspired all who knew him. A devout Catholic, he was a member of Prince of Peace Catholic Church for over 30 years. He was born in Pittsburgh, Pennsylvania, graduated from North Catholic High School in 1955, and proudly served in the United States Navy.

He then attended and graduated from Florida State University, where he met his wife, Margaret. An avid sports fan, he coached and officiated for many years and was a father figure and mentor to many young people. He was preceded in death by his parents, Aloysius and Sophia Lewandowski, his brother, George Lewandowski, and sisters, Joan Lynch and Karin Marcil.

His memory will live on in the hearts of his devoted wife of 46 years, Margaret Toney Lewandowski, his son, Michael Lewandowski (Dixie), his daughters Donna Krusbe, Sharon Gutteridge (Lee), Elaine Daniels (Guy), and his 13 grandchildren: Courtney, Justin, Ryan, Kayla, Chase, Connor, Clare, Eric, Teresa, Kara, Matthew, Lindsay, and Lauren.

Ski's wife, Margaret, passed away ten months later, in November 2010. Both are buried in Jacksonville, Florida.

BIBLIOGRAPHY

Beckles, Gordon. *The Bridport Story (1253 to 1953)*. London: Harrison and Sons, LTD.

Burton, Kathryn. *Old Lyme, Lyme, and Hadlyme*. (Images of America). Charleston, SC: Arcadia Publishing, 2003.

Schuler, Stanley, ed. *Hamburg Cove: Past and Present*. (Lyme's Heritage Series). Old Lyme: Lyme Historical Society and Florence Griswold Museum, 1995.

Smith, Annie Morrill. *Morrill Kindred in America*. New York: The Lyons Genealogical Company, 1914.

Encyclopedia Britannica online: www.britannica.com
Naval History Website: www.history.navy.mil
Online maps: www.worldatlas.com
Wikipedia

PHOTOGRAPHS

The Sweet Shop in Tallahassee, Florida, as it was in the 1960s.

The Sweet Shop today.

BJ's parents, Bob Minnick Sr. and Nedra Louise Alexander,
August 1935.

Nedra and Bob Minnick, 1940s.

Nedra with her sons, Bruce and BJ at the farmhouse in Bull Hill, Connecticut.

BJ's grandparents Guy and Edna Minnick, with their sons Bob and John, 1920s.

Edna and her boys (clockwise from lower left): Don, John, Bob Sr., and Bruce.

The Minnick brothers (clockwise from top left): Bob Sr., John, Don, and Bruce.

*The Minnick family
home on Clover Drive
in Great Neck, Long
Island, New York,
during the summer and
winter, 1920s.*

*John and Bob Minnick
playing soldier, 1920.*

*Royal Dutch at Bull Hill,
1941.*

Boot camp at U.S. Naval Training Center, Waukegan, Illinois.

BJ, around the time when he joined the Navy.

ENLISTED CLASSIFICATION RECORD

LAST NAME	(Middle)	SERVICE NO.	RATE	CLASS	CO. NO.	D.O.T. OCCUP. CODE
MINNICK ROBERT JR		4782480	SR	13389	000,000

YR. BIRTH	GCT	ARI	MECH	CLER	SONAR	
38	54	49	49	45		

TEST SCORE PROFILE

	GCT	ARI	MECH	CLER	SONAR
HIGH 1					
2					
AVER 3	X	X	X	X	
4					
LOW 5					

SPECIAL TEST SCORES

NAME	FORM	DATE	SCORE
Radio	2	8/15/55	65

MOST SIGNIFICANT EDUCATION	DATES	YEARS EDUCATION	DEGREE	NAME OF COLLEGE OR UNIVERSITY
High School	9/52-6/55	11		

MAJOR COURSES		SPECIAL STUDIES	ALG., GEOM.	TRIG	PHYS.	TYPING	SHORTHAND
General		HIGH SCH.	1			WPM	WP
SPECIALIZED TRAINING (Vocational, trade, technical, business)		COLLEGE				WPM	WP

LEISURE TIME ACTIVITIES	SPORTS IN WHICH QUALIFIED
Hunting(small game) - Spear Fishing	

TALENT FOR PUBLIC ENTERTAINMENT	HIGHEST POSITION OF LEADERSHIP

MAIN CIVILIAN OCCUPATION (D.O.T. TITLE)	EMPLOYER'S NAME
STUDENT	

LOCATION	YRS. SERVICE	WKLY. WAGE	TRADE TEST NAME	SCORE

DUTIES, SKILLS, MACHINES

SECOND BEST OCCUPATION (D.O.T. TITLES)	EMPLOYER'S NAME

LOCATION	YRS. SERVICE	WKLY. WAGE	TRADE TEST NAME	SCORE

DUTIES, SKILLS, MACHINES

OTHER WORK EXPERIENCE

RIGHT EYE	CORR.	LEFT EYE	CORR.	RIGHT HANDED	LEFT HANDED	QUALIFIED SWIMMER	QUALIFIED FOR	NOT QUALIFIED FOR
20/20		20/20		X		3 CLASS		

RECOMMENDATIONS AND REMARKS
3-90-30

RECOMMENDED TO STRIKE FOR	Finished File Pers-E224
Electronics Operator Ratings	

PREPARING ACTIVITY	I VOLUNTEER FOR	INITIALS
USNTC, GREAT LAKES, ILL.	CT Duty	RW

INTERVIEWER'S SIGNATURE	VERIFIED	DATE
Robert Wood Minnick	V. R. BERSIE, PNC, USN	8/16/55

ENLISTED CLASSIFICATION RECORD   NAVPERS-601 REV (8-50)

BJ's enlistment record for boot camp in Great Lakes, Illinois.

The Imperial Beach Basic Class 13D-56(R), February 1956.
FRONT ROW: *Mert Janovec, Cedar Bluffs, NE; Bob Critchfield, IN;
J. P. Wright, CTC, Instructor; Robert Burchell Jr., MI; and Paul
Humler, Albany, NY.* SECOND ROW: *Mike West, AR; Tom Livsey, Dickson
City, PA; Donald Detwiler, Stillwater, OK; [?] Miller, NJ; Robert Taylor,
NC; Chuck Svymbersky [?], Peoria, IL; and unknown.* THIRD ROW:
*Dave Wright, NH; James Logsdon, Mount Sterling, IL; Lonnie
Urick [?], Omaha, NE; Ray Frazelle, Peoria, IL; Richard Wood, TX;
Martin Brooks, OR; Bob Minnick Jr., FL; Chuck Harrelson, Fort
Myers, FL; and Bob Baker, KS.* (Photo courtesy of Chuck Harrelson, CTIC
USN Ret.)

Imperial Beach (IB) Advanced Class 13C-56(R), May 1956.
TOP ROW, LEFT TO RIGHT: *Stater, Rowland, Asleyman, Wood, Wantiez, Collins, Logsdon, Harrelson, Minnick, Baker, West, and Speckhals.*
MIDDLE ROW: *Hail, Lewandowski, McManus, Tishauser, Cater, Smith, Snodgrass, Page, and Livsey.* BOTTOM ROW: *Humler, Walde, CTC Rice (Instructor), Reindorf, and Detwiler.* (Photo courtesy of Jerry Lail)

Entering Imperial Beach, California, 2018.

Imperial Beach pier, 2018.

Imperial Beach "Spy School," 1950s.

Neeb and Ski at CT School in Imperial Beach, 1956.

Neeb playing quarterback with (LEFT TO RIGHT) *Ski, Swanson, and Seimonson in front, at Imperial Beach, 1956.*

The AN/FRD-10A circularly disposed antenna array (CDAA) "elephant cage," 2002.

*The barracks and classrooms at the Imperial Beach "Spy School." (*Photo courtesy of Don Hayes)

Top Secret clearance for CNO cryptographic from March 19, 1956.

Navy Occupation and Training History, 1955–1957, Imperial Beach.

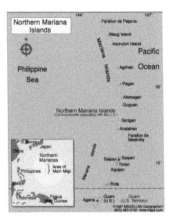

Maps of Guam and the Mariana Islands.

BJ on Guam, 1957.

The launch of
Sputnik *by the*
USSR, 1957.

The USS Virgo
returning to
San Diego
from Guam,
early 1950s.

CHARLESTON
AIR FORCE BASE
3311

On the way to North
Africa, 1958.

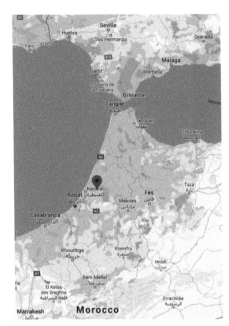

Map of Algeria.

Location of Sidi Yahia, Morocco.

BJ, center, and friends in a bar in Sidi Yahia, North Africa, 1958.

The bus route from Casablanca to Tangier, then on to Gibraltar, where BJ saw Caterina Valente.

Caterina Valente.

Valente's recording of "The Breeze and I," 1955, which reached number 13 on the charts.

BJ heard about Buddy Holly's plane crash around 7:00 to 7:30 a.m. on February 3, 1959, while in North Africa.

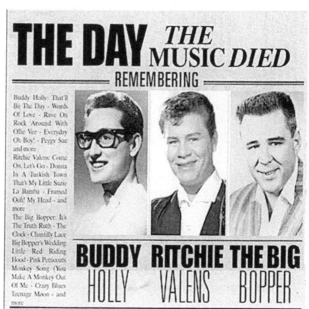

Balaklava, in the Black Sea, where a secret USSR submarine base was located.

The Balaklava submarine pens were underground, hidden from military trawlers' view.

An RAF camouflaged RD4 used during World War II, the same type that was used in the desert camel tracks.

A Convair B-58 Hustler (top speed: 1,358 mph) was used for providing cover and protection in the Sahara.

Charles de Gaulle in 1942.

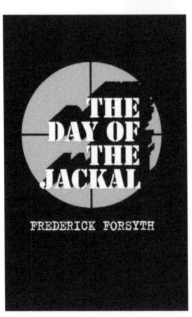

First edition of The Day of the Jackal, *1971.*

U.S. NAVAL COMMUNICATION FACILITY
NAVY NUMBER 214
c/o Fleet Post Office, New York, N.Y.

2465-600/CCW;ga
P15
Serial: 1003

MAY 8 1959

From: Commanding Officer, U.S. Naval Communication Facility, Navy 214
To: MINNICK, Robert W., Jr., 478 24 80, CT3, USN

Subj: Letter of appreciation

Ref: (a) HD, NAVSECGRU ltr ser 00059P30 of 13 April 1959

1. Reference (a) is a letter of appreciation to this command based on a memorandum from the Chief of Naval Operations commending the Naval Security Group
for its contribution to a special operation of prime importance and significance. It is quoted in part:

"1. The contributions of the Naval Security Group in support of this operation attest to the importance of the work it is doing and to the skill and
devotion to duty of its personnel.

2. It is requested that you convey to those directly involved my heartiest congratulations and my appreciation for a job well done.

/s/ Arleigh Burke"
ARLEIGH BURKE

2. Along with the commendation from the Chief of Naval Operations, and the
personal "well done" of the Head, Naval Security Group, I wish to add my appreciation for your personal contribution and devotion to duty which made this
operation successful. This reflects great credit upon the Naval Security Group
Department of this command, and is in keeping with the highest traditions of
the Naval Service.

3. A copy of this letter will be entered in your service record, and in the
case of officers, also forwarded to the chief of Naval Personnel.

M. J. SMITH

*Commendation letter from Chief of Naval Operations, Admiral
Arleigh Burke, for a job well done, which protected de Gaulle
from another assassination attempt, May 8, 1959.*

Fidel Castro, John F. Kennedy, and Nikita Khrushchev, the main players in the Cuban Missile Crisis of 1962.

John F. Kennedy addressing the nation on the missile crisis.

Fidel Castro with Nikita Khrushchev.

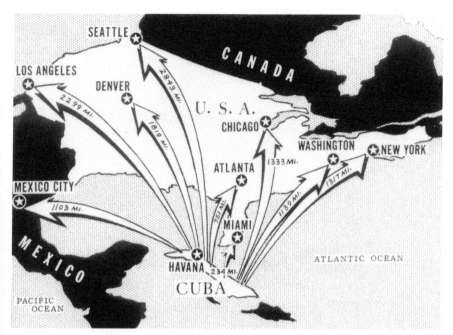

A map showing the distances of major cities from Cuba, which illustrated the imminent threat of nuclear war.

American and Russian military vessels headed for a standoff during the missile crisis.

*BJ, in retirement, reminiscing on the beach
about his Navy career, 2012.*

*BJ's daughter, Mimi Minnick, and son,
John Minnick, 2012.*

ACKNOWLEDGMENTS & THANKS

CAROL WILSON: Retired teacher, Blountstown Public Library patron, and member of the Calhoun Library Board. Carol was a real friend to Bob Minnick, and helped him daily to express his ideas on paper—clearly and with grammatically correct phrases and punctuation. Thank you, Carol.

DARLENE EARHART: Head of the Blountstown Library's computer lab. Darlene provided support to Bob whenever he needed it—technical or otherwise. She made sure he had a dedicated computer and space to work on his memoir. Thank you, Darlene.

HARMON BRODY: Blountstown Library patron and friend to Bob. He provided a sounding board for political ideas, as well as much needed encouragement. Thank you, Harmon.

RITA MAUPIN: Director of the Calhoun County Public Library System. Rita was also a sounding board for Bob, listening to and encouraging him. Additionally, she provided Bob's collaborator, Lindy Minnick, with valuable information about all the people that supported Bob in his memoir project, as well as a colorful description of how Bob spent his days at the library. Thank you, Rita.

MIKE REDELA: Bob's grandnephew. Mike helped with proof-reading in the early stages of the manuscript's creation. Thank you, Mike.

And a special thank-you to all of Bob's friends and family who supported his quest to provide a memorable book about his time in the Navy during those tense Cold War days.

ABOUT THE AUTHORS

Robert Wood Minnick Jr. (JULY 12, 1938–JUNE 18, 2018)

Bob (BJ) was born in Plainfield, New Jersey, to Robert Wood Minnick and Nedra Louise Alexander, who met while enrolled at the University of Michigan at Ann Arbor. In 1941, BJ's father went to work for Shell Oil Company—testing fuels for submarines at General Dynamics Electric Boat Division in New London, Connecticut. Robert Sr. moved the family to Hamburg Cove, on the banks of the Connecticut River, where BJ and his younger brother, Bruce Alexander, were raised until 1947, when the family moved to Fort Lauderdale, Florida.

In 1955 BJ joined the United States Navy and became a Naval Intelligence operative (CT3), serving two two-year tours of duty on the island of Guam and in North Africa. Following his two tours in the Navy, in 1964 BJ graduated from Florida State University's School of Business with a bachelor's degree in business and finance.

BJ enjoyed a lucrative career in Florida commercial banking, moving up the ladder to the top very quickly. He served as vice president of the Pan American Bank, N.A., in Miami;

executive vice president of the Citizens National Bank in Orlando; and president of the Guaranty National Bank in Tallahassee. BJ retired from commercial banking in the late 1990s and created a consulting firm designed to assist the different kinds of financial institutions then undergoing the financial upheavals of that era. He continued consulting into his mid-seventies.

BJ had a passion for sport fishing. He enjoyed fishing in deep waters, trolling for game fish in the Gulf Stream off the coast of Fort Lauderdale and in the Gulf of Mexico. His secret dream—expressed only to close family—was to move to the Florida Keys and operate a small charter boat business catering to Wall Street bankers and others who loved deep sea fishing.

BJ met Mary Alice Leonard while they were attending FSU. They were married in 1964 in Blountstown, Florida, and celebrated their golden wedding anniversary in 2014. BJ and Mary Alice had two children: Mary Louise Minnick (Mimi) and John Alexander Minnick. Mimi and John and their children still reside in north Florida—close enough to the Gulf Coast to enjoy the salt air smell and the snow-white sand beaches.

BJ began working on his Cold War memoirs with his cousin, Lindy Minnick, in 2016, continuing until his death in Blountstown in 2018.

Marian Lindsey (Lindy) Minnick (1944–)

Lindy was born in Washington, D.C., to John Bradley Minnick and Frances Mackell Shears. She grew up in Arlington, Virginia, and graduated in 1968 from George Washington University's Columbian College, with a degree in philosophy.

Lindy moved to California in 1973 and continued a forty-five-year career in computer hardware and software technical sales as a systems analyst. She was with Honeywell Information Systems for seventeen years on both the East and West Coasts; and then worked for Silicon Valley– and Boston-based companies, including Tandem, Wang Labs, Novasoft, Documentum, and EMC/Dell.

Lindy retired in Hemet, California, in 2010, and pursued genealogy and family-history memoir writing. She currently resides in San Marcos, California, with her ginger cat, Sunshine. Lindy has two sons: Mike Redela, who lives in Encinitas, California, and Tony Yemma, who lives in San Francisco, as well as two grandchildren: Averi and Shane Redela.

Lindy published her father's memoirs, *Wishing Stones and Rubber Ice*, in 2012, and is writing a third family memoir, *Letters from Belize*, about her uncle Bruce Morrill Minnick (1917–1999).

LEFT TO RIGHT: *The cousins, Bob Jr. (BJ) and Lindy Minnick; BJ with his dad, Bob Sr., in Great Neck, New York, 1939; and Lindy with her dad, John, in Grace Park, Pennsylvania, 1946.*

CPSIA information can be obtained
at www.ICGtesting.com
Printed in the USA
LVHW030937230222
711817LV00005B/141